BRADWELL'S LONGER WALKS ON
DARTMOOR

JOHN NOBLET

BRADWELL
BOOKS

Published by Bradwell Books
9 Orgreave Close Sheffield S13 9NP
Email: books@bradwellbooks.co.uk

All rights reserved. No part of this publication may be reproduced, stored in a retrieval system or transmitted in any form or by any means, electronic, mechanical, photocopying, recording or otherwise without the prior permission of Bradwell Books.

British Library Cataloguing in Publication Data: a catalogue record for this book is available from the British Library.

1st Edition

ISBN: 9781910551639

Print: CPI Group (UK) Ltd, Croydon CR0 4YY

Design by: Mark Titterton

Typesetting by: Mark Titterton

Photograph Credits: © John Noblet

Maps: Contain Ordnance Survey data
© Crown copyright and database right 2016

Ordnance Survey licence number 100039353

The information in this book has been produced in good faith and is intended as a general guide. Bradwell Books and its authors have made all reasonable efforts to ensure that the details are correct at the time of publication. Bradwell Books and the author cannot accept any responsibility for any changes that have taken place subsequent to the book being published. It is the responsibility of individuals undertaking any of the walks listed in this publication to exercise due care and consideration for the health and wellbeing of each other in the party. Particular care should be taken if you are inexperienced. The walks in this book are not especially strenuous but individuals taking part should ensure they are fit and able to complete the walk before setting off.

CONTENTS

Walk 1	**Belstone Tor and the East Okement Valley** 10 or 7 miles / 16 or 11.5km	p.6
Walk 2	**Meldon Reservoir and the King Way** 6 miles / 9.5km	p.12
Walk 3	**Dartmoor's Highest Tors** 9½ miles / 15km	p.18
Walk 4	**Lydford and Great Links Tor** 12 miles / 19km	p.24
Walk 5	**Wheal Betsy and the River Tavy** 9½ or 6 miles / 15 or 9.5km	p.30
Walk 6	**Postbridge, Bellever and Pizwell** 9 miles / 14.5km	p.36
Walk 7	**Dartmeet, the Coffin Stone and Two Rivers** 8½ miles / 13.5km	p.42
Walk 8	**Buckfast Abbey and Hembury Woods** 9 miles / 14.5km	p.48
Walk 9	**Harford and Western Beacon** 10 miles / 16km	p.54
Walk 10	**Roborough Down and Shaugh Bridge** 9 or 6 miles / 14.5 or 9.5km	p.60
Walk 11	**Burrator Reservoir and Sheeps Tor** 10½ or 7½ miles / 17 or 12km	p.66
Walk 12	**Ringmoor Down and Drizzlecombe** 8 miles / 12.5 km	p.72
Walk 13	**Princetown, Swell Tor and Crazywell Pool** 9½ miles / 15km	p.78
Walk 14	**Ten Tors Challenge the Easy Way** 9½ or 6½ miles / 15 or 10.5 km	p.84
Walk 15	**Buckland Beacon and Rippon Tor** 6 miles / 9.5km	p.92
Walk 16	**Haytor Down** 6 miles / 9.5 km	p.98
Walk 17.	**Hound Tor and Bowerman's Nose** 7 miles / 11km	p.104
Walk 18.	**Grimspound and Hamel Down** 8 miles / 12.5km	p.110
Walk 19.	**Castle Drogo and Cranbrook Castle** 7½ miles / 12km	p.116
Walk 20.	**Fernworthy and Chagford Common** 8½ or 7 miles / 13.5 or 11 km	p.122
About the Author		p.128

INTRODUCTION

There is nowhere quite like Dartmoor. It is, perhaps, the most varied of England's National Parks and can be many things to many people.

This is not just another book of walks on Dartmoor. The circular walks have been selected to provide a broad overview of the rich and varied landscape that is Dartmoor. These new walks are between 6 and 12 miles in length; shorter walks can be found in *Bradwell's Walks For All Ages on Dartmoor*. In addition to the detailed route directions, the author has provided lots of additional information to add to the interest and enjoyment of walking on Dartmoor.

Dartmoor is the highest land south of the Peak District and the central moor can be a bleak and trackless place but magnificent in its own rugged way. The high moor is the source of many of Devon's rivers and there are no fewer than eight reservoirs. As those rivers make their way to the sea, some flowing north and others south, they have carved their way through steep-sided wooded valleys past picturesque hamlets and villages.

Four thousand years of history are there to be explored. Alongside Bronze Age stone rows, stone circles and hut complexes, there are tinners' workings from the Middle Ages and later 19th-century industrial remains to be seen on almost every walk.

Some of the tracks across the moor are hundreds of years old. Several connected the pre-Reformation abbeys at Tavistock, Buckfast and Buckland whilst others linked the Stannary towns of the medieval tin-mining industry. The Abbots Way, the Jobbers' Path and the Lych Way can still be followed. They are marked by ancient bridges and wayside crosses and shown on Ordnance Survey maps.

The trees in a few of the ancient woodlands are estimated to be hundreds of years old, whilst other rare species of plants and insects are to be found only on Dartmoor. The iconic Dartmoor pony roams freely and buzzards and skylarks are a common sight overhead. Dartmoor is also rich in legends and folklore and many of the stories are centuries old. Most have some basis in fact whilst others require a little imagination.

The walks in this book aim to show this diversity but in a way that is easy to follow and without the need for serious navigational skills. Most walks are on tracks and paths or on open moor where there are prominent landmarks. Walkers are, however, reminded that the upland areas of Dartmoor are open and exposed and care needs to be taken.

In particular:
- Stout footwear, preferably proper walking boots, is essential.
- Dartmoor acts like a sponge and gets more than its share of rain, over 2,000mm (80 inches) in a year. Tracks can be wet underfoot, particularly if it has rained recently.
- The weather conditions can change rapidly. In all but the most settled conditions waterproofs should be taken.
- Although most of Dartmoor is 'open access' land, i.e. there is 'a right to roam', some areas remain privately owned and there may not be a right of access. Dartmoor is still very much a working environment, especially farming and the military.
- Walkers must be aware that there are three areas of Dartmoor that are used by the military for training purposes. These are clearly marked on OS maps as 'Danger Areas' and access is sometimes restricted. Details are published in advance and red flags are flown. Only Walk 3 in this book is within such an area, but others are close.
- Mobile phone coverage is generally poor.
- Satnav postcodes are given for the start point of each walk. However, as Dartmoor is sparsely populated these are often only approximate. Grid references are also provided.

1 BELSTONE TOR AND THE EAST OKEMENT VALLEY

A VERY VARIED WALK STARTING AT OKEHAMPTON STATION AND FOLLOWING THE EAST OKEMENT RIVER UP ONTO THE MOOR. AFTER CIRCLING BELSTONE COMMON ON OLD MILITARY TRACKS WE REACH THE VILLAGE OF BELSTONE BEFORE RETURNING ON THE DARTMOOR WAY.

From the station, now a summer heritage railway, the walk descends to Okehampton's Simmons Park before turning upstream alongside the East Okement River. The river tumbles down through oak woods from high on the moor before joining the River Torridge which reaches the sea at Bideford.

The going is easy apart from a couple of rocky sections on the riverside as the path passes a series of waterfalls and it is for this reason that the walk is graded Moderate/Hard. The climb up to Belstone Common is straightforward and with splendid views deep into the moor.

We visit the Nine Maidens stone circle, probably a burial site dating from the Bronze Age. From here the route uses some of the many military tracks on this part of the moor. The military have trained on Dartmoor for over 200 years and Okehampton Camp, less than 2 miles away, is still an important military tactical training base. The camp was originally established for artillery training and many miles of tracks, commonly known as military roads, were built for the movement of horse-drawn weaponry and carts.

Turning north our route takes us along the valley of the River Taw with Belstone Tor (479m or 1,571ft) on the left and Cosdon Hill (550m or 1,804ft) on the right. On the way we pass the remains of the Irishman's Wall. One of the ancient customs of Dartmoor was

BRADWELL'S LONGER WALKS

that certain tenants had the right to enclose common land, i.e. build a wall. Although there is more than one version of the story, the usual one is that a group of Irishmen were employed to build a wall. This upset the locals and they waited until it was almost finished and met in force to destroy large parts of it. What is left has been known as Irishman's Wall ever since.

Belstone is mentioned in the Domesday Book and, at 300m (1,000ft) above sea level, is one of the highest villages on Dartmoor. On the green are the village stocks and the animal pound whilst the simple granite church is worth a visit.

The return is by field footpaths and then an easy track back to Okehampton Station.

THE BASICS

Distance: 10 miles / 16km or 7 miles / 11.5km

Gradient: Mostly easy gradients but a short steep section on the riverside path

Severity: Moderate/Hard

Time: 4½ hours or 3½ hours

Stiles: Three

Map: OS Explorer OL28 (Dartmoor)

Path description: Riverside and field paths, moorland tracks and a short distance on lanes

Start point: Okehampton Station visitor centre (GR SX 592944)

Parking: Free car park on the south side of the station (EX20 1EW)

Dog friendly: Yes, if they can manage the stiles and on leads if near animals on the moor or on public road

Public toilets: Seasonal toilets for public use on Okehampton Station

Nearest food: Seasonal café on Okehampton Station and The Tors Inn at Belstone

Shorter walk near here: Walks for All Ages on Dartmoor - Walks 7 and 8

1 BELSTONE TOR AND THE EAST OKEMENT VALLEY

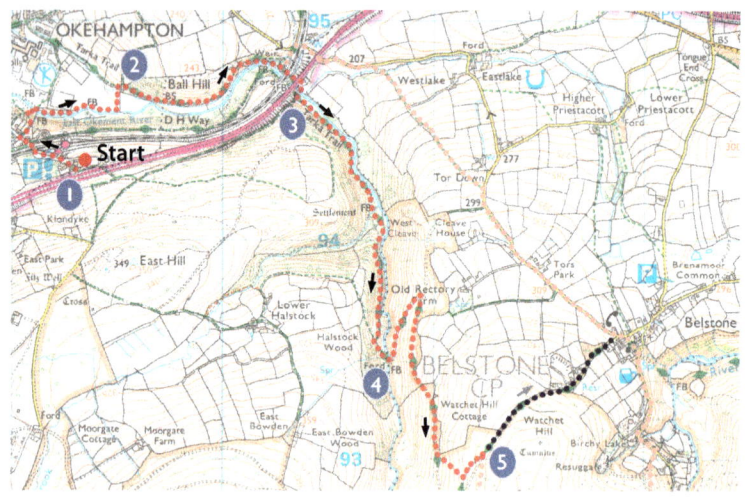

The Route

1. Turn right out of the car park to go under the railway bridge and past the entrance to the station. Walk down the hill for 50m and turn right onto a footpath signed for the town centre via Simmons Park. The path descends steeply to a junction. Go straight on, down a few steps which are rather slippery and worn, signed to the town centre via Riverside and then right at the next junction, also signed to the town centre, down more uneven steps. At the bottom cross the bridge over the East Okement River and then go immediately right into Platt Meadow. Walk up the riverside path around the school playing fields ignoring a wooden bridge on the right.

2. Go over the footbridge in the corner and turn right to a gate into Ball Hill conservation area. Follow the path for half a mile (800m) walking at first alongside a leat that supplied water to the Town Mill (an old corn mill in Okehampton which can still be seen), and then beside the river.

Go through the gate at the end and turn right, signed to Fatherford. Pass through another gate and under the stone Fatherford railway viaduct to cross the river on Charlotte's Bridge. The bridge was named after 12-year-old Charlotte Saunders who sadly drowned whilst trying to cross the river in 2001.

3. Turn left, signed as a footpath to the East Okement Valley. The path goes under the concrete viaduct carrying the A30 trunk road. It then follows the river upstream through mixed woodland of oak and other broadleaved trees.

   Shortly after a rather rocky part, which can be slippery, bear left on the waymarked footpath over a footbridge crossing the Moor Brook. Walk through the oak trees and through a gap in the wall opposite and then continue alongside the East Okement River. There is then another rocky, and possibly slippery, section as the path climbs up with a series of waterfalls below. The final stretch, by the largest waterfall, can be treacherous if wet, so take care.

4. Cross a footbridge and go left on a broad track which soon starts to climb steadily through gorse and bracken as views of North Devon open up ahead.

   Turn right at a path junction onto a grassy path heading towards a field wall. The path keeps close to the wall to pass the ruin of Watchet Hill Cottage. Where the path forks, go left towards the highest point of Belstone Tor. The path is rather faint but curves to the left to meet a more obvious stony track. Go left and walk gently uphill towards a field wall on the left. Just before the wall a broad grassy track joins from the right.

   If you wish to do the shorter option, continue onward on the track which soon goes through the moor gate and drops down into Belstone on a tarmac lane. At the old telephone box continue the walk from Waypoint 10.

1 BELSTONE TOR AND THE EAST OKEMENT VALLEY

5. Otherwise go sharp right, almost doubling back, on the grassy track towards trees in the middle distance with Oke Tor beyond. After 200m or so this brings us to the stone circle known as Nine Maidens (although shown as Nine Stones on the map). Why this is called Nine Maidens is one of Dartmoor's mysteries as there are many more stones than nine. It is said that if you count them you will get a different number each time. The legend here (as for some other stone circles) is that the maidens were turned to stone for dancing on a Sunday.

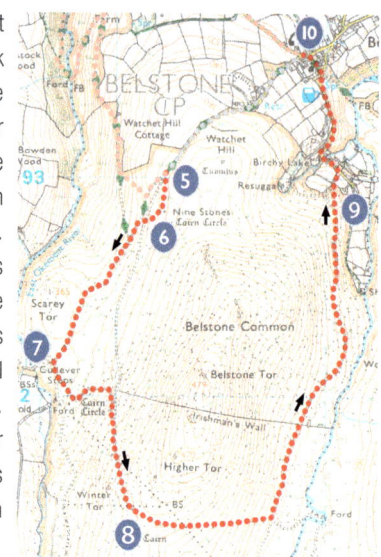

6. From here take the wide grassy path going downhill. Cross a rough track and continue in the same direction to meet a good stony track in a shallow cutting. This is one of the military tracks and the gentle gradient and easy curves are evidence that they were built with wheeled wagons and gun carriages in mind.

7. Turn left downhill towards the river. Before reaching the river bear left at a fork and almost immediately afterwards go left again to take the track back up towards Winter Tor.

8. Pass Winter Tor on your right and 100m further on take the left fork. Keep on this grassy track which may be indistinct in places but goes straight across the ridge which separates the Okement and Taw valleys. Just off the path to the left is Higher Tor and boundary stones marking the parish boundaries of Belstone and Lydford. On the right is Taw Marsh with Steeperton Tor in the middle distance (with the military lookout hut on top) and beyond this to the right is Fur Tor on the skyline, the most remote tor on Dartmoor.

Continue on this path steadily downhill to reach a good military track above a ford crossing the River Taw. Bear left and follow this military track for 1 mile (1.6 km) passing the remains of Irishman's Wall on the way to arrive at a gate.

9. Beyond the gate the tarmac lane goes down to the hamlet of Birchy Lake with an interesting collection of abandoned farm machinery on the roadside. As the village of Belstone is approached there are splendid views across Belstone Cleave and the valley of the River Taw. Go left at the fork to pass The Tors public house where you might like to stop for refreshment.

10. At the old telephone box (which now contains a defibrillator) you can turn right if you wish to visit the village green just 100m down the road. The village stocks and an old pound are close to the memorial commemorating the Coronation of King George V on one side and the Coronation and two Jubilees of Queen Elizabeth II on the other. Otherwise turn left and immediately take the right fork. Continue on this lane for just over half a mile (1 km).

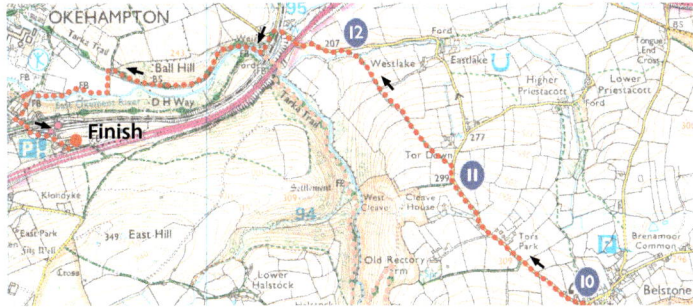

11. Cross a cattle grid and immediately go left over the stile and onto the footpath signed to Fatherford. Go diagonally across the field to a gap in the opposite hedge and then go downhill with the hedge on the right to a second stile. Continue downwards, but with the hedge now on the left to cross a third stile. Notice the old slotted gateposts on either side of the path. At the bottom cross a small stream on a stone clapper bridge to reach a kissing gate onto a lane.

12. Turn left and walk along the lane under the noisy A30 and a railway bridge. Go left down the hill, ignoring the right fork, and signed as a bridleway. At the end of the lane go through the gate just before the railway viaduct that we saw earlier. Cross Charlotte's Bridge again but this time turn right to go back under the viaduct and through another gate. The path veers to the left and continues along the top of the meadow with the river below. The very easy gradient is because this was a horse-drawn tramway dating from 1870 built to serve a quarry near the viaduct.

Go through two gates, turn left at the road and go back under the railway bridge to reach the parking area.

2 MELDON RESERVOIR AND THE KING WAY

A walk from Meldon Reservoir follows the West Okement River through oak woods carpeted with bluebells in spring and then climbs gently to the open moor along the ancient King Way. The end of the walk is along the southern side of the lake.

After crossing the Meldon Reservoir dam, constructed in 1972 and the last reservoir to be built on Dartmoor, we follow the valley downstream. Then we pass an old quarry of geological interest as a source of aplite and other rare minerals. The route continues under the graceful structure of Meldon Viaduct, a wonder of late Victorian railway engineering. It was built of wrought and cast iron in 1874 for the London and South Western Railway main line from Plymouth to Exeter and Waterloo and was originally single track. The track was widened in 1878 by building an almost identical viaduct alongside. Partly because of the exposed position it has had to be strengthened three times before becoming today's cycle track.

After walking through oak woods we cross the river on a wooden footbridge before a short and steep climb up to a track which follows the route of the historic King Way. The common theory is that the King Way was an early road between Tavistock and Okehampton and then on to Exeter by which the king's mail was carried before the turnpike era and is probably named in honour of King Charles I. However, it is doubtless much older in origin, possibly Saxon, as it keeps to the high ground over the moor.

After reaching the hamlet of Meldon we go under an old stone railway bridge and continue easily up onto the open moor with splendid views to the north and south. On one side the

Devon countryside stretches away with the Cornish hills beyond and on the other are the highest tors of Dartmoor, Yes Tor and High Willhays.

The route descends to cross the West Okement River on a footbridge and then the way back is alongside the reservoir. There is the option to take a short diversion to follow a track upstream from the end of the reservoir to visit Black-a-Tor Copse. This is one of Dartmoor's ancient woodlands and is a National Nature Reserve. It is considered one of the best examples of high-altitude oak woodland in Britain and the mosses and lichens which cover the boulders and trees are rare indeed.

THE BASICS

Distance: 6 miles / 9.5km

Gradient: Easy gradients but one short steep section

Severity: Moderate

Time: 2¾ hours

Stiles: None

Map: OS Explorer OL28 (Dartmoor)

Path description: Paths, possibly muddy in places, tracks and a quiet lane

Start point: Meldon Reservoir (GR SX 561918)

Parking: Car park at the reservoir with honesty box (near EX20 4LU)

Dog friendly: Yes, but on leads if near animals on the moor or on public road

Public toilets: At start

Nearest food: Sourton A30 services (1 mile)

Shorter walk near here: Walks for All Ages on Dartmoor - Walk 10

2 MELDON RESERVOIR AND THE KING WAY

The Route

1. Turn left out of the car park down the roadway to the dam and cross to the far side. There are views over the reservoir to the high point of Corn Ridge on the right and on the other side there are views down the valley of the West Okement River to the splendid Meldon railway viaduct.

   Go through the metal gate and turn left through a second (wooden) gate. Take the path ahead ignoring side paths to the left and right to walk along the hillside towards the viaduct. This path meets a broad track and descends to an old quarry.

2. The track crosses a concrete bridge over the Red-a-ven Brook beyond which are a few remains of some old buildings, including a weighbridge. There is not much to show for the fact that there were several industries here. The quarry was a source of aplite, a fine-grained granite which has a number of uses, one of which  was the basis of glassmaking. Grand plans for large-scale glass manufacture in the 1920s turned into a financial disaster but the quarry continued until the 1970s. Further up the Red-a-ven Brook was a small-scale copper mine whilst higher up still is a small reservoir that provided Okehampton with much of its water supply at one time.

Pass through a wooden gate and up to the road which leads to a much larger quarry, a major source of railway ballast until it closed in 2011. Turn left onto the road for just 25m before bearing right on a path signed as a public footpath to Rock Park.

After just a few metres bear left, again signed as a public footpath and left again shortly after. Behind is West Mill Tor (541m or 1,719ft high) whilst to the left can be seen the dam that we crossed and a second quarry to the right of the river. This was for limestone and there are lime kilns nearby.

As the path enters the woods, go right at a junction. Shortly afterwards the path passes underneath the viaduct and it is easy to see how this was originally a single track line and the second viaduct was built immediately beside it. You can, if you wish, climb the steps on the right up to the top of the viaduct to admire the views over the valley.

Continue on this path through the woods, ignoring several side turnings, until it meets the tarmac access road by a small parking area. This ancient woodland, mostly English oak but some beech and hazel, is spectacular in May with a complete carpet of bluebells. Other seasons are a delight with ever-changing colours.

3. Cross the road and take the path in the left corner of the parking area which is, for a short distance, beside the busy A30 trunk road. At this spot the A30 is almost at the highest point in all of its 284 miles between London and Land's End.

Soon the path bears left and we quickly leave the road to walk upstream alongside the West Okement River passing a number of small waterfalls on the way. Look out for woodpeckers and the unusual horseshoe bracket fungi on some of the dead tree trunks. Pied flycatchers arrive in spring and although dormice are here in good numbers they are nocturnal and you will be very lucky indeed to see any.

4. At a substantial wooden footbridge cross the river and bear left steeply uphill through the oak woods. The pain is short and sharp as the path climbs away from the river to reach a gate.

Go sharp right onto a wide track and through a gate at Meldon Farm. This route is part of the old King Way and you will notice an old milestone by the steps opposite the entrance to the farm.

Carry on along the track, now concrete, to pass the village hall. Go left on the lane in front of a row of old cottages.

5. Pass under an old railway bridge and continue straight on at the T-junction signed to the moor. After the entrance to Higher Bowden House the lane continues as a bridleway.

Go through a gate and carry on alongside the hedge to reach a second gate. Views open up to the right towards North Devon and the Cornish hills 25 miles away.

2 MELDON RESERVOIR AND THE KING WAY

6. At a bridleway post opposite a metal gate and just before a row of trees turn left onto a grassy track. However, if you walk forward for another 100m or so to the gate beside the line of trees you will be able to see the outline of Sourton Tors ahead. On the hillside are a series of ridges and depressions and these are the remains of another unusual Dartmoor industry. In the 1870s there was a business here manufacturing ice. The pools were filled with water from a spring which then froze in the winter weather. The ice was cut into blocks and stored in trenches before being transported to Plymouth for use by the fishing industry.

Follow the track towards Yes Tor (with the flagpole) across the valley, almost the highest point on Dartmoor at over 2,000 feet (619m). Go around a fenced area to drop steadily towards the end of the reservoir. This is a fine view of the relatively small reservoir. When full, its deepest point is 42m (140 feet) and it can hold 300 million litres (65 million gallons) of water.

The track rounds a sharp left and then a sharp right bend and continues downhill with a fence on the left. Steps lead down to an old stone bridge below but ignore these and continue on the main track.

7. At the bottom, go through a gate immediately after a sharp left-hand bend and cross the stream to stay on the track. There is a ford here but just below there are places where the stream narrows and it is easy to step across.

    A few metres after the ford go right on a broad grassy track to a substantial concrete footbridge over the West Okement River, avoiding some rather boggy stepping stones. Cross the river and continue ahead to a broad track.

    To extend the walk to Black-a-Tor Copse, turn right up the broad track for half a mile (800m). The copse is one of three ancient oak woodlands on Dartmoor and is designated as a National Nature Reserve. The trees are very old and stunted by the poor soil and inhospitable climate. However, the woodland supports one of the best examples of upland lichen communities in Britain which cloak the oak trees set among massive moss-covered boulders. Several species of nationally rare lichens grow here.

8. Otherwise turn left to follow the path which veers around to the right. On the left is the old stone bridge at Vellake Corner that we saw from above earlier and then we pass beside a small footbridge. Continue ahead and as the path climbs above the waters of the reservoir it becomes more rocky underfoot. Follow this path around the lake and back to the dam. Turn left over the dam and back to the car park.

3 DARTMOOR'S HIGHEST TORS

Dartmoor is sometimes called the last wilderness in England and much of the upland northern moor is a wild and rather featureless landscape with few tracks and paths. This walk includes several of the highest tors including High Willhays and Yes Tor, both over 2000 feet (600m) above sea level. There is no higher land in the whole of southern England.

The walk makes use of old military roads to go to the more remote parts of the moor. It is a way of being able to experience Dartmoor's highest tors and a wilderness almost untouched by human hand without the need for serious navigation skills. Having said that, this walk should not be undertaken in poor visibility. Although it is mostly on the military roads, some is on open moorland and, in any event, there would be no point – this walk is all about the views.

The military have used Dartmoor as training ground since the time of Queen Victoria. A training camp was established in the 1890s and many miles of tracks, known as military roads, were constructed for the movement of horse drawn artillery. Some remain in use today because Okehampton Camp is still a military training facility. For this reason the public are not allowed access at certain times and you must make sure that there are no red flags flying before setting out on the walk.

It is a steady climb up from the start but it is not steep. On the way we pass a disused military target railway.

From the high point the walk crosses open moorland, which may be wet underfoot, to Dinger Tor. There is no clear path, but the terrain is a gentle downhill gradient and the

rocks of the tor are clearly visible ahead. At Dinger Tor we rejoin the military roads to cross the valleys of the Black-a-ven Brook and then the infant East Okement River towards Steeperton Tor and the valley of the larger River Taw.

After walking close to one of the old military observation posts the route continues along the ridge that divides the Okement and Taw rivers. Passing Oke Tor and Winter Tor there are splendid views across Taw Marsh to Cosdon Beacon. Another military road takes us over Cullever Steps where the Black-a-ven Brook and the East Okement meet on their way down to Okehampton and the sea at Bideford.

THE BASICS

Distance: 9½ miles / 15km

Gradient: Some ups and downs but not steep. The first 2½ miles is all uphill.

Severity: Moderate/Hard. This walk is partly on open moorland, rough in places, and should not be attempted in poor visibility.

Time: 4¾ hours

Stiles: None

Map: OS Explorer OL28 (Dartmoor)

Path description: Stony military tracks and some open moorland. Several small streams to cross.

Start point: Roadside parking area above Okehampton Camp (GR SX 596923)

Parking: From Okehampton town centre follow signs to Okehampton Camp (EX20 1QP). After 1 mile pass the entrance to Okehampton training camp, go over a small bridge and up the hill for nearly a mile to a parking area at the top where the track forks.

Dog friendly: Yes, but on leads if near animals

Public toilets: None

Nearest food: Various cafés and pubs in Okehampton town centre

Shorter walk near here: Walks for All Ages on Dartmoor - Walk 9

NOTE: This walk is within the Okehampton Military Range Danger Area. You must check beforehand that no live firing is taking place. You can do this online by putting 'Dartmoor Firing Programme' into your search engine or phoning 0800 458 4868. Red flags are flown from various points, including Yes Tor, if public access is not permitted.

3 DARTMOOR'S HIGHEST TORS

The Route

1. Walk away from the parking area and take the right fork on the track into the moor. There are views from here in every direction. The long ridge of Belstone Tor is on the left. Rowtor is the closest tor on the right and further away is Yes Tor, both of which have military flagpoles.

   Note: If the flags are flying you should not be here!

2. After about 500m go right at a fork and here the climb up to Dartmoor's highest point starts. There is nowhere else in the south of England higher than 2,000ft (610m) above sea level. West Mill Tor soon comes into view ahead and just after this there are some old rifle butts on the left. Beyond them, about 200m away, you will see the embankment and engine house of the old military

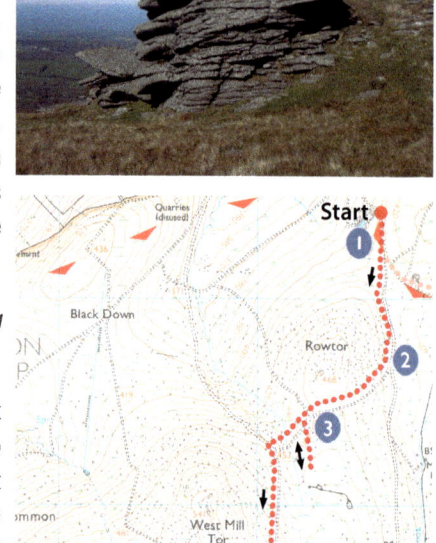

   target railway. Targets were attached to an unmanned self-propelled trolley along a length of narrow-gauge track about 200m long with a turning loop at both ends. To have a closer look at this go left across the moor on a minor track opposite the point where another track comes in from the right.

3. Otherwise continue straight on and down to a ford over the Moor Brook. Go left at the T-junction after the ford and continue onwards and upwards with West Mill Tor on the right. Bear right at the next fork and, as the track climbs upwards, Yes Tor appears ahead with the smaller profile of High Willhays to the left. It is one of Dartmoor's illusions that, from whichever direction it is viewed, Yes Tor will always appear to be the higher summit. Indeed, it was believed for many years to be the highest point on Dartmoor until modern surveying equipment determined that High Willhays is, in fact, just 2 metres (6 feet) higher.

4. After crossing another small stream the track steepens before levelling out and ending abruptly just after rounding a corner. Take the faint grassy path on the left and after just a few more metres turn right on a cross path towards Yes Tor and climb up to the summit.

There can be no better view on a clear day. Looking north, over a substantial Bronze Age cairn, is the slender Meldon Viaduct way below, built to carry main line trains in the 1870s. The North Devon countryside stretches towards Exmoor in the distance. To the west, over the deep valley of West Okement River is Great Links Tor and far away are the hills of Bodmin Moor. To the east is the rounded shape of Cosdon Hill whilst to the south is the wide open space of Dartmoor stretching towards the English Channel.

5. Retrace your steps and take the clear path towards High Willhays. This is a rather disappointing and unimpressive scattering of rock piles after Yes Tor and does not really do justice to the fact that this is the highest point on Dartmoor. The pile on the left with the cairn on top is the actual highest point.

From the last rock pile, almost conical in shape, take the faint grassy path across the moor in a south-easterly direction for just over 1km (¾ mile) to Dinger Tor. The path is not clear but keep as straight as possible to avoid the rough tufty grass on either side. This part of the walk can be wet underfoot and so care is needed.

3 DARTMOOR'S HIGHEST TORS

6. At Dinger Tor the views are true wilderness. Apart from a couple of military lookouts on the right there is almost no sign of any human interference and just a few ponies and sheep. In the distance Fur Tor is a prominent lump on the skyline almost due south.

   You will need a vivid imagination to believe that once upon a time a giant called Blunderbus lived there with his favourite wife, Jennie. It's a convoluted story but she fed him a wonderful food known as clouted cream. This has become the clotted cream for which Devon is rightly famous.

   Walk away from the tor up the military track. As the gradient levels out the profile of Steeperton Tor comes into view with Oke Tor just below the horizon.

7. Bear right at a fork and go downhill. This is easy going to a sharp bend at the head of the Black-a-ven Brook at the bottom. Go up the other side and cross a tarmac track to keep straight on towards Steeperton Tor.

8. The next section of track is very rocky and care is needed. At the bottom cross another stream. Beyond this the trail, once again smooth and grassy, bends to the right and as it does so one of the military observation posts can be seen below Oke Tor.

9. Cross another tarmac track and a further stream before going straight uphill. The pathway has been eroded by run-off rainwater and it may be better to walk to one side of it for a while.

   When the path levels out there is another observation post on the right, looking rather like a small tor. The River Taw lies in the valley ahead and if we were to continue down we would arrive at a ford crossing the river at a place known as Knack Mine Ford. In this remote spot there was a small tin mine known as Wheal Virgin. There are records of its existence as long ago as 1799 and it was producing tin on and off until about 1880. There are a few ruins still to be seen.

10. However, to continue the walk turn left here, before starting to go downhill towards Steeperton Tor. Take the clear path towards Oke Tor which soon joins the Knack Mine Track. Carry on along the ridge and pass to the right of Oke Tor. Views across Taw Marsh open up with Belstone Tor ahead.

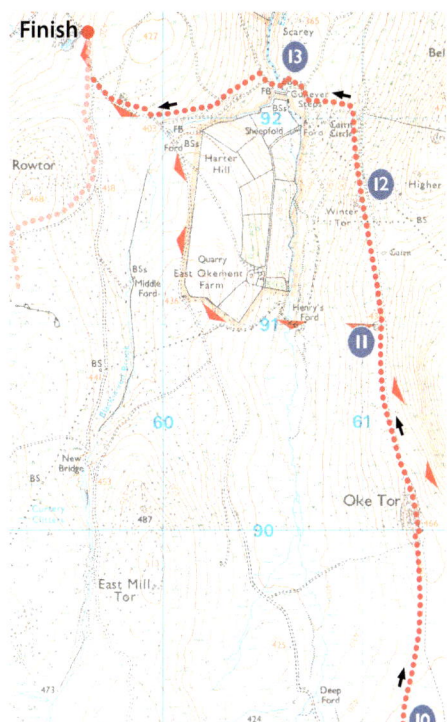

11. Continue onwards, passing the red-and-white military range boundary poles by the diminutive Knattborough Tor, and the top of Winter Tor appears to the left of the path. Follow the good wide track, bearing left at a fork to pass alongside the tor.

12. Continue down another rather rocky section of military road. Go round a left-hand corner and straight on at the next bend (cutting off the corner) to rejoin the track just before Cullever Steps. There are two bridges here, alongside which are both fords and stepping stones. The fords

are paved with granite slabs put there to take the weight of heavy horse-drawn gun carriages. The confluence of the two rivers is just below Cullever Steps before they flow down to Okehampton. There the East and West Okement rivers meet before joining the Torridge and flowing north to the Bristol Channel.

13. Cross the bridges and notice a very tall boundary stone on the left with a much smaller one beside it. They mark the boundary of the parishes of Okehampton and Belstone. Carry on up the hill on the track, keeping straight on at a junction. Turn right when you meet the tarmac road and back to the parking area.

4 LYDFORD AND GREAT LINKS TOR

THIS WALK IS AN EASY WAY TO GET TO THE TOP OF GREAT LINKS TOR, THE HIGHEST ON THE WESTERN SIDE OF DARTMOOR. FROM THERE WE GO TO WIDGERY CROSS, A LANDMARK FOR MILES, WHICH SITS HIGH ABOVE THE SAXON VILLAGE OF LYDFORD.

Lydford has a history dating back many centuries. Long before the Norman Conquest the Saxon kings of Wessex had founded a settlement here, the remnants of which are still visible. It must have been an important place, as a mint was established in the 10th century and some coins from this era are on display in the Castle Inn.

The Normans built a fort but the castle we see today was constructed in about 1200 as a prison. In medieval times Lydford had jurisdiction over the tin-mining areas of Dartmoor. The Stannary prison had a grim reputation and 'Lydford Law' was notorious. An old poem from the 17th century ran: 'I've oft heard of Lydford Law, where in the morn they hang and draw, and sit in judgment after.'

Lydford Gorge is just half a mile away. Here the River Lyd has carved the deepest gorge in the south-west and there is a 30m (100ft) waterfall. The gorge is in the care of the National Trust and open to the public (except in winter).

Soon after leaving the village the route crosses Fernworthy Down to join the Granite Way before reaching open moorland at Nodden Gate. It is a steady climb on the track of the horse-drawn Rattlebrook Peat Tramway up to Great Links Tor. This imposing tor is 586m (1,922ft) above sea level.

BRADWELL'S LONGER WALKS

From Great Links we go to Brat Tor, somewhat lower but a landmark because of the massive cross on the summit. The cross was erected in 1887 by William Widgery to mark the golden jubilee of Queen Victoria and is the largest of many granite crosses on the open moor. William and his son Frederick are arguably the best known of all Dartmoor artists and William lived in Lydford for some years.

It is impossible to go anywhere on the moor without coming across remnants of lost industries. Having walked up the old tramway for the peat industry our path takes us from Brat Tor to High Down Ford over the River Lyd and past ruined buildings of 19th-century tin workings. An old green lane brings us under a disused railway and back to Lydford.

THE BASICS

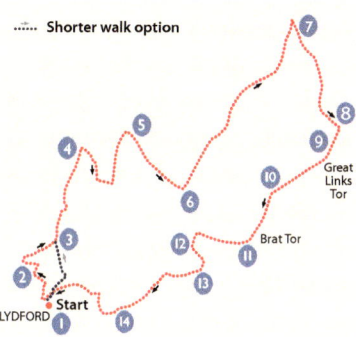

..... Shorter walk option

Distance: 12 miles / 19km
Gradient: Easy gradients but a long climb to Great Links Tor
Severity: Moderate. This walk is partly on open moorland and should not be attempted in poor visibility.
Time: 5¾ hours
Stiles: None
Map: OS Explorer OL28 (Dartmoor)
Path description: Paths, tracks and lanes, some open moorland. May be muddy near start, especially after prolonged rain.
Start point: Lydford free car park (GR SX 510847)
Parking: Lydford free car park, opposite Castle Inn (EX20 4BH)
Dog friendly: Yes, but on leads if near animals on the moor or on public road
Public toilets: At start but closed in winter
Nearest food: Castle Inn, Lydford or café at National Trust Lydford Gorge (seasonal)

4 LYDFORD AND GREAT LINKS TOR

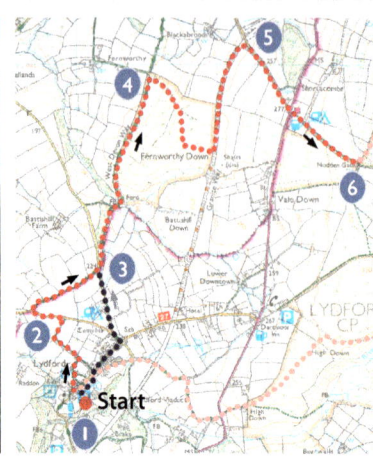

The Route

NOTE: The first section of this walk can be very muddy after prolonged rain. If in doubt, take the alternative road route to Waypoint 3.

1. Cross the road from the car park and walk up the Saxon lane signed as a public bridleway beside the Castle Inn. Pass two old stone buildings and then the ancient spring. Go left at a junction, pass a house on the left and bear right at the next fork to meet a lane.

2. Go left and walk along the road for 250m before turning right on a green lane signed as a public byway. This old track can be muddy after rain.

   Alternative route: Turn right out of the car park and walk up the road, past the village hall to the war memorial. Turn left and immediately fork right (signed Watergate) for ¼ mile (400m) to Waypoint 3.

3. At a road junction by a white house continue on the byway which now becomes a sunken lane descending through trees to a path junction. Go right and through a gate to cross a stream on an old stone clapper bridge. Bear left as the path climbs up onto Fernworthy Down and the views open up on both sides.

4. Just before a field wall and a large metal gate turn right onto a broad but faint grassy path under the telephone wires. Go steadily uphill keeping the gorse thicket on the left.

   Continue ahead at a minor path junction and at the top of the rise pause to admire the views of the ridge that we will walk later. Ignore any side paths to reach a metal gate onto the Granite Way, formerly the old railway line from Plymouth to Exeter and Waterloo. Turn left and after 600m the Granite Way meets a lane.

5. Turn right up this road lined with beech trees for 300m to the main A386 by the Fox & Hounds Hotel. Cross carefully – it is a busy road. Go up the stony track beside the

pub. At the top there are two gates with a boundary stone indicating the parish boundaries of Bridestowe and Lydford. Pause to enjoy the views behind with Brent Tor's distinctive conical shape and church on the top.

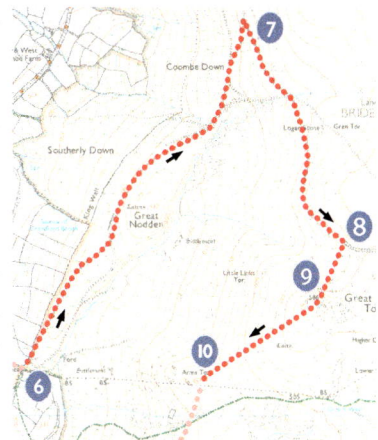

6. Go through the left-hand gate and bear left onto a track immediately past the covered reservoir. Shortly the track splits and we bear right away from the wall towards the rounded hill that is Great Nodden.

The path meets another track emerging from a cutting. This is part of the Rattlebrook Peat Tramway and the marks of the sleepers which carried the rails are clear to see. The horse-drawn tramway was built in 1879 to bring peat from high on the moor to Bridestowe station.

There now follows a long climb although the gradient is very easy. The reward is great views across Lake Viaduct and deep into mid Devon. (Lake is an old Devon word for a hamlet, not an expanse of water.)

7. Go sharp right at a tramway junction. This is where there was a small siding allowing the peat trucks to negotiate a zigzag. Continue on the tramway now heading towards Great Links Tor and cross the infant River Lyd on an embankment.

8. The track enters a shallow cutting and just as it starts to go around a left-hand bend take a faint grassy path leading to the right of the rock piles of Great Links Tor. The ground is very peaty underfoot (and may be wet in places) before ascending steeply to the summit. Climb up towards the right where the trig point is visible.

It is worth stopping to savour the views here. Towards the east is Fur Tor, the most remote tor on Dartmoor, whilst Great Mis Tor is to the right of the communications mast on North Hessary Tor. Further right the sea at Plymouth Sound should be visible together with Caradon Hill (with the two masts) on Bodmin Moor.

9. From the west side of the highest point and with the trig point on the left go south towards one of the smaller rock outcrops that is part of Great Links Tor. Go to the right of this and then take the grassy path towards Arms Tor below.

10. There are several rock piles, not a single outcrop, and the route takes us to the left of these to continue forward on a rather vague grassy path towards Brat Tor. The path swings in an arc to the left (to avoid old tinners' workings and rough ground in the dip).

4 LYDFORD AND GREAT LINKS TOR

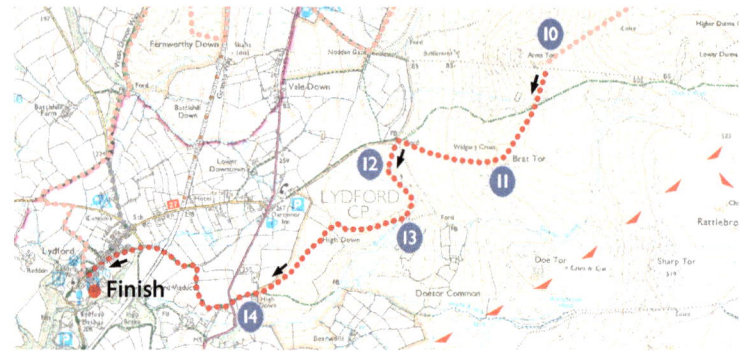

11. In contrast to the older crosses on Dartmoor, the one on Brat Tor is not cut from a single mass of granite but is built up from a series of blocks, presenting a rather unusual appearance. Go to the right of the tor and here a broad grassy path drops steeply down before levelling out in the valley bottom at a footbridge (or stepping stones if you prefer) to cross the River Lyd.

12. Turn left and follow the riverside path. There are several small pools and little waterfalls along here. One of the pools is known as Witches Pool and is underneath a rocky outcrop called Black Rock. There is a bench and above it a memorial to a First World War soldier. Captain Nigel Hunter was killed in action in France in 1918, aged just 23, and the memorial plaque includes a poem that he wrote on his last visit to Dartmoor.

The path, which is rather rough and rocky in places, follows the river to meet a track by an old ford. The ruined building is another reminder of the mining era.

Wheal Mary Emma was a small tin mine that operated around 1850 on both sides of the river.

13. Go right up the track and carry straight on at a grassy junction. Bear left at another junction towards a boundary wall and a row of beech trees. Follow the wall to a wooden gate by a substantial house. Go through the gate and into an old green lane known as Skitt Lane.

14. At the bottom, cross the busy A386 with care to continue on Skitt Lane past two houses. Follow the lane going sharp left at a junction and, a little later, under an old railway bridge.

Carry straight on at a path junction by a white house and up the track into Silver Street. Go left past Nicholls Hall and back to the car park. Just past the telephone box is a gate on the right where the Saxon town banks are clear to see.

Before you leave Lydford take time to look around the castle, owned by English Heritage but entry is free. The church is mostly 13th century and is known particularly for two things: firstly, the splendid woodwork, especially the bench ends, but also the 'watchmaker's tomb' from 1802, the epitaph of which starts 'Here lies in horizontal position the outside case of George Routleigh, watchmaker'. It continues in whimsical fashion ending that he hoped to be 'thoroughly cleaned and repaired and set going in the world to come …'

5 WHEAL BETSY AND THE RIVER TAVY

A varied walk, combining open moorland with great views, followed by a waterside walk though woodland. Wheal Betsy is notable as being the only surviving mine engine house on Dartmoor.

The walk starts close to the National Trust property of Lydford Gorge. This is the deepest gorge in the South West and has a 30m (100ft) high waterfall called the White Lady. We then cross two railway bridges, a reminder of the fact that the small village of Lydford, which dates back to Saxon times, once had two railway stations and which, oddly enough, were side by side.

There is a view towards Brentor Church high on the top of Brent Tor as we cross Black Down and then climb to the top of Gibbet Hill. There was indeed a gibbet here and criminals were left to die in the full sight of passers-by on the Tavistock road as a deterrent to others. There is a splendid outlook in all directions with the western tors of Dartmoor, the sea at Plymouth and the Cornish hills all clearly visible on a fine day.

This is mining country and the nearby Wheal Friendship was a hugely successful copper mine which finally closed just before World War I after more than 50 years' production. There were several other smaller mines in the area. These included one on Gibbet Hill itself, Wheal Betsy and Wheal Jewell and we pass all of these sites. There is not much to see today apart from

the Wheal Betsy engine house, the only one left on Dartmoor. This mine was moderately successful in the 1860s and 1870s but for silver and lead rather than copper and tin.

The water that powered these mines was brought from the River Tavy, by means of water channels known as leats. Two of these leats are still in use today supplying water to the Mary Tavy hydroelectric power station. This was built in the 1930s and at one time was the largest in England.

We then pass the Wheal Jewell reservoir and walk through Horndon, once a busy mining community but now a quiet backwater. An old green lane brings us to the Hill Bridge Leat and we walk for nearly a mile along this old waterway to Hill Bridge itself and the River Tavy, which is said to be the second fastest-flowing river in England. It is an easy walk with wide open views across Kingsett Down before going gently back to the start.

THE BASICS

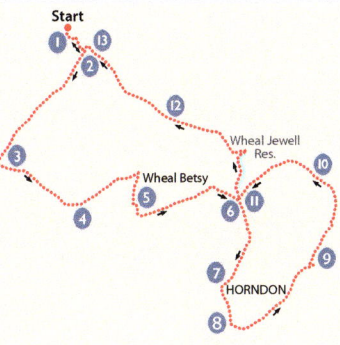

Distance: 9½ miles / 15km or 6 miles / 9.5km

Gradient: Easy gradients but one longish climb to Gibbet Hill

Severity: Moderate

Time: 4¾ hours or 3 hours

Stiles: Two

Map: OS Explorer OL28 (Dartmoor)

Path description: Mostly moorland tracks, a waterside path and a quiet lane

Start point: Lydford Gorge White Lady NT car park (GR SX 501832)

Parking: Lydford Gorge White Lady NT car park (EX20 4BL)

Dog friendly: Yes, if they can manage the stile and on leads if near animals on the moor or on public road

Public toilets: At start

Public toilets: Toilets for public use at start but closed in winter

Nearest food: National Trust café at start, closed in winter

Shorter walk near here: This walk can be shortened to 6 miles by going straight on at Wheal Jewell reservoir (Waypoint 5) and following the route from Waypoint 11.

5 WHEAL BETSY AND THE RIVER TAVY

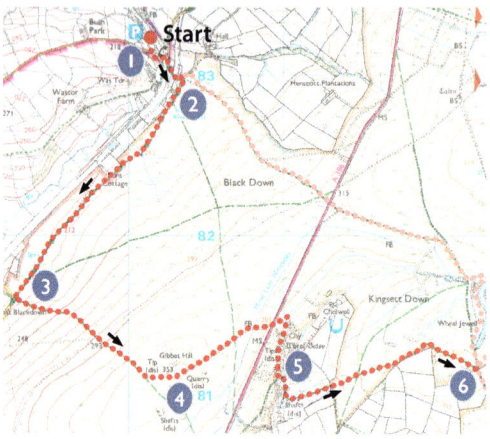 

The Route

1. Turn left out of the car park, go past the Mucky Duck and cross the old railway bridge. Turn right after the bridge, signed as a public bridleway. (The Mucky Duck was once a thriving public house beside the railway and you may notice on the roadside verge an old Great Western Railway (GWR) boundary marker dated 1895).

   Bear left up the slope and over a second railway bridge. There was a time when the small village of Lydford had two railway stations and was served by two different companies, the Great Western Railway and the London and South Western Railway. Times have changed and the only public transport link today is an infrequent bus to Tavistock!

2. Go through the gate and immediately right to walk alongside the fence. This may be muddy for a short distance, but as the path rises to pass under telephone cables it becomes firmer. The church on the top of Brent Tor comes into view ahead as several small streams are crossed. Continue on the now grassy path in the direction of Brent Tor passing a boundary stone marking the parishes of Mary Tavy and Brentor.

3. The path meets a lane by another boundary stone. Turn left up the broad grassy path to climb steadily up Gibbet Hill, ignoring any side paths. The climb is worth the effort because at the top is a splendid Dartmoor skyline of tors. The most identifiable ones include North Hessary Tor with the communications mast, Cox Tor and Great Mis Tor. Turn left at this point towards the spoil heaps of an old quarry and the summit of Gibbet Hill with its trig point.

   From here the views are tremendous. Dartmoor stretches away to the north and east whilst to the south beyond the fenced-off shaft of an old mine is Tavistock.

On a clear day the sea at Plymouth is easily visible as are the Cornish hills on Bodmin Moor to the west.

4. Walk away from the trig point half right in a north-easterly direction and almost immediately the chimney stack of the Wheal Betsy engine house and a white farmhouse come into view. (Do not take the wide path heading north towards Great Links Tor and the A386 road).

Cross the course of a dried-up leat that supplied water to the mine on Gibbet Hill to reach a gate beside the A386. Cross the road carefully and go through the furthest left of three gates and down a track beside the post and wire fence. At a path junction turn sharp right down the rocky track to the engine house. There is a plaque on the wall, giving some of the history.

5. Continue past Wheal Betsy and down the track. This is stony at first but becomes very rocky towards the bottom and care is needed. Go left on the concrete track, over the Cholwell Brook and almost immediately right through a gate signed as a bridlepath. Go up the slope away from the stream to a metal gate. Just beyond the gate is a fenced-off mine shaft, one of several in the area. Keep straight ahead up the track to pass a small conifer plantation on the right and, at the top, a stone field wall. When the wall ends continue straight on towards a rather ugly concrete building. This is Wheal Jewell reservoir. Water from Tavy Cleave flows along an old leat which originally served mines in the area, including Wheal Betsy and the one on Gibbet Hill which we have passed, and is now piped from here to the Mary Tavy hydroelectric power station.

5 WHEAL BETSY AND THE RIVER TAVY

6. Go down the track to reach a road. Bear right past a row of former miners' cottages then over the cattle grid and past an old chapel, with a huge monkey puzzle tree. This small hamlet of Horndon was once a busy mining community and boasts an old pub with a most unusual name. The Elephant's Nest is just 300m down the road.

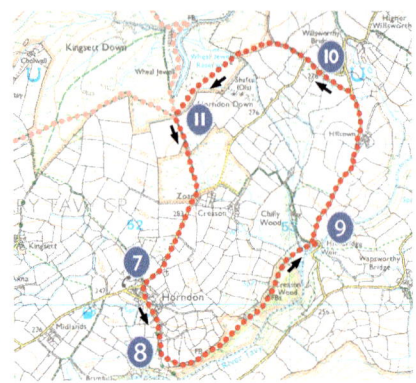

7. However, to continue the walk turn left at the T-junction by the post box and pass some more old buildings. Turn left again at a second junction past Furzemans Farm. The tarmac lane ends and becomes a rough green lane as it descends into the Tavy valley.

8. After about 150m the track crosses the Hill Bridge Leat. Go left here over the stile to walk upstream towards Hill Bridge itself. There is a second stile and a couple of gates as the path meanders through the woodland with the River Tavy audible at first and then visible in the valley below.

9. After almost a mile the leatside path arrives at Hill Bridge and the weir where the water is taken from the River Tavy. The modern, and rather out-of-place, concrete and metal structures in the river are all to do with the protection of migrating salmon. Go sharp left beside the weir up the steep slope to the road (or up the metal ladder if you prefer).

   Go left up the lane and round a sharp bend. Further on, look out for a rather challenging stone stile on the left signed as a public footpath but this can, thankfully, be ignored. Continue past Hilltown Farm and bear left at a road junction signed for Horndon. Go straight on at the next junction. All the while there are views over the hedges towards Tavy Cleave, considered by many to be one of the most picturesque river valleys on the moor.

10. Where the lane goes sharp left continue straight ahead on a green lane signed as a public bridleway. At the top of this rocky track go through the moor gate and bear left on the path alongside the wall.

    Go through a gateway and past another fenced-off shaft up the grassy track, now bearing away from the wall on the left towards the Wheal Jewell reservoir building to a stony track.

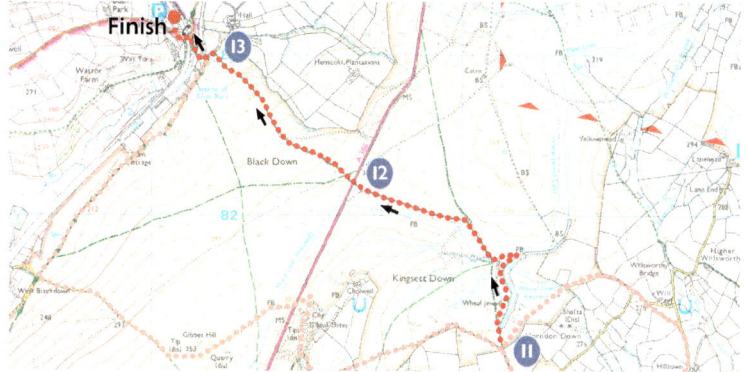

11. Turn right on the track, pass the reservoir building and go immediately right behind the building to reach the track which runs alongside the reservoir. Go left, with the water on the right. Cross a bridge and pass a second before reaching the end and a path junction. Go left and then take the second of two tracks on the right that are close together (and opposite a retaining wall of an older reservoir). After 250m bear left again towards the road which you can now see and hear. There are several paths but continue to follow the lower one with a series of small timber posts as markers.

12. Go through the gate and carefully cross the A386 again. Go half right after crossing the road alongside a post-and-wire fence across the moor. After about 650m there is a staggered junction but keep going forward towards the prominent white house that we passed early in the walk. There is no real track but this is easy moorland walking.

13. Turn left at the bottom where there is a bridleway sign and go through the gate beside the white building. From here, return to the car the same way as the outward route.

6 POSTBRIDGE, BELLEVER AND PIZWELL

Postbridge is about as close as you can get to the geographical centre of Dartmoor on a main road. With a river, an ancient clapper bridge, a large car park and a village shop, it is no surprise that it is a very popular spot.

The medieval clapper bridge probably dates from the 13th century, when Postbridge was on the route from this part of the moor to Tavistock, one of the tinners' Stannary towns. The bridge is, without doubt, the finest example of its type to be seen on Dartmoor. Although there are many other clapper bridges, and we will pass two more on this walk, Postbridge is the largest and most complete. Incidentally, the 'modern' road bridge beside it is itself almost 250 years old, having been built in the 1780s.

This walk soon leaves the camera-happy trippers behind to head south through Bellever Forest to Bellever Tor. This is one of the highest tors on the southern side of Dartmoor and the views are outstanding in all directions.

Leaving Bellever Tor we make our way to Dunnabridge Pound. This was once one of the most important animal pounds on the moor. Its use as a pound probably dates from the 14th century, but it is thought that the site may originally have been a Bronze Age enclosure. It would have been used to impound animals that were rounded up by the bailiffs of the Forest of Dartmoor because they were grazing illegally on Duchy land. Just inside the

BRADWELL'S LONGER WALKS

gate is a huge slab of granite forming the pound keeper's shelter. Tradition has it that this came from Crockern Tor, the site of the ancient tinners' Stannary Parliament.

After passing the few remains of Brimpt's tin mine we pass a massive standing stone at the head of a stone row. There are several stone rows and hut circles in the area, but many are difficult to locate because of the vegetation.

At Bellever Bridge there is another ancient clapper bridge, although less complete than that at Postbridge. Following the route of the Lych Way we then pass through the ancient hamlets of Pizwell and Lower Merripit. Pizwell is one of the seventeen Ancient Tenements of the Forest of Dartmoor, first mentioned in documents in 1260. The present buildings date from the 16th century, as do those at Lower Merripit.

THE BASICS

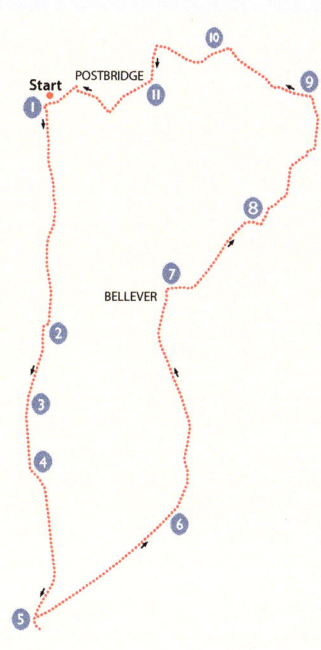

Distance: 9 miles / 14.5km
Gradient: Easy gradients
Severity: Moderate
Time: 4½ hours
Stiles: One
Map: OS Explorer OL28 (Dartmoor)
Path description: Mostly good moorland and field tracks with short distance on road. Can be muddy in places.
Start point: Postbridge visitor centre car park (GR SX 647788)
Parking: Dartmoor National Park car park. Honesty box (PL20 6TH)
Dog friendly: Yes, if they can manage the stile and on leads if near animals on the moor or on public road
Public toilets: At start
Nearest food: East Dart Hotel at Postbridge. Several pubs and cafés in Princetown.
Shorter walk near here: Walks for All Ages on Dartmoor - Walk 12

6 POSTBRIDGE, BELLEVER AND PIZWELL

The Route

1. Go through the gap in the wall at the top end of the car park by the visitor centre. Turn left and then cross the road with care. Go through the gate beside the cattle grid and immediately right into Bellever Forest, signed as a public footpath. Then bear left through a wooden gate and up the forestry track.

   Follow a series of wooden marker posts with a yellow stripe, ignoring any side turnings. Eventually the track leaves the forest and Longaford and Higher White Tor are glimpsed to the right and soon Bellever Tor appears ahead. When the main track veers to the left carry straight on towards the tor, which now dominates the skyline.

2. Go through an old gateway and continue ahead on the wide grassy path to the summit. However, about halfway between the gateway in the wall and the top of Bellever Tor you may be able to make out the old walls of a large prehistoric settlement just a few metres from the path.

   Bellever Tor is 443m or just short of 1,500ft above sea level and the 360-degree views are tremendous.

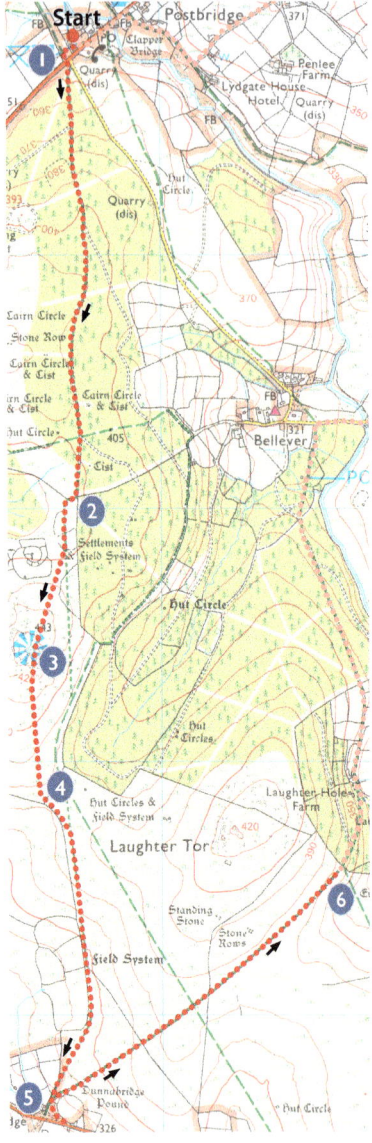

This is the highest point for miles around and straight ahead is the ridge of Holne Moor whilst to the left are Haytor Rocks and Rippon Tor. In the opposite direction can be seen the communications mast on North Hessary Tor and Beardown Tors further to the right.

3. From the summit continue onwards in the same direction. At first this needs some care as the path drops down through the clitter (rocks and boulders) surrounding Bellever Tor. It soon becomes a clear grassy path heading towards a field wall.

4. Go through the gate in the corner and bear right alongside the wall. This grassy path, possibly muddy in places, has wide open views towards the Holne Moor ridge and with the valley of the East Dart River below. Go through another gate and soon the Princetown to Dartmeet road and the roofs of Dunnabridge Farm come into view. Approaching a further gate the substantial wall of Dunnabridge Pound is on the left.

5. To enter the pound, and possibly take a breather on the ancient canopied seat, sometimes known as The Judge's Seat from its connection with the Stannary Parliament, go through the gate and turn left for a few metres to the entrance gateway. Once inside, the sheer size of the pound is impressive and it is hard to imagine how many animals could have been held here.

Go back to the gate and take the right fork alongside the pound wall signed as a bridlepath to Laughter Hole Farm. This stony track goes gently uphill through two more gates before levelling out. There you will see two fenced-off mine shafts on the right. These were part of Brimpts Mine, which was producing tin in the mid-19th century. The underground workings were up to 50m (165ft) below ground.

Shortly after the mine shafts there is a path crossing and on the left is a prominent menhir, or standing stone 2.4m (8ft) high. This marks one end of a rather incomplete stone row, difficult to find in the gorse and heather, probably because many of the stones have found their way into the nearby farm walls! Also on the left, beyond the standing stone, are the stone walls of an old sheep pound in front of Laughter Tor. This curiously named tor is a derivation of Lough Tor, the name by which it used to be known.

The long, and relatively flat, ridge ahead is Hamel Down, to the right of which are the distinctive twin humps of Haytor Rocks whilst further right, and closer, are Yar Tor and Sharp Tor.

6 POSTBRIDGE, BELLEVER AND PIZWELL

6. Continue onwards and pass through a gate signed as a bridlepath to Bellever. Ignore the fork to the left and continue straight on down the hill to reach another gate and the farm buildings of Laughter Hole Farm. Laughter Hole is a crossing point over the East Dart River by means of stepping stones and you may be able to hear the river from here. After ¾ mile (1.1km) the track descends to go through another gate at the bottom into a forestry plantation beside the river.

7. Turn right at the road to go over Bellever Bridge. There is an old clapper bridge on the right. It is similar to, but not quite as large as, the one at Postbridge. The river crossing here is on the route of the Lych Way. This ancient track owes its origin to the fact that prior to 1260 local people were obliged to carry their dead to Lydford for burial. Farms such as Pizwell, which we will soon walk past, were in the parish of Lydford despite the fact that Widecombe is much closer.

Follow the road up the hill to pass a stone inscribed with the letter C. This denoted the limit of the county's responsibility for maintaining the bridge and such stones are often to be found near Dartmoor's larger bridges. Around 100m after this, look out for a faint grassy path on the left at the end of the gorse thicket (but

40

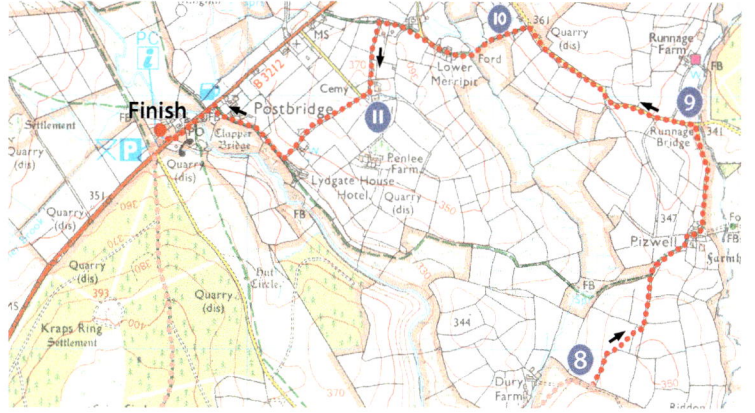

beware, there is no footpath sign). The path descends towards a stream with old field walls beyond. It then follows the stream to reach a farm track leading to Dury Farm. Turn right up the track and after 175m look out for a ladder stile on the left beside a gate and signed to Pizwell.

8. Walk alongside the wall on the right and then bear half right across the field to a track in the corner of the field. Go left, signed as a path, to descend between walls to reach a gate in a wall built of very large stones.

   Pass a collection of derelict farm machinery and through another gate to reach Pizwell. The footpath goes between the ancient buildings. Turn left onto the tarmac access track to Runnage Bridge.

9. Turn left here and walk along the lane for half a mile (0.8km). Take care as there may be traffic on this road, which leads to Widecombe. There is, however, a wide verge on the right for most of the distance to a cattle grid. Go through the gate beside the cattle grid and immediately left on a track towards a bungalow.

10. Turn left through the gate and down the track signed as a public bridlepath to Postbridge. Cross a stream on an ancient clapper bridge to reach Lower Merripit Farm through gates on either side of the yard.

    Pass Lower Merripit Cottage on the left and take the left fork just afterwards where, again, there is no sign. After 150m turn left on a permitted bridlepath opposite a timber garage building and beside the entrance to Broad Down.

11. Turn right at the end of the path to pass Postbridge cemetery and then straight on down a lane to Higher Lydgate Farm. At the end go through a gate into a rather rocky ancient green lane. Turn right at the bottom, signed as a path, to reach the main road beside the East Dart Hotel. Turn left to cross the bridge and back to the car park.

7 DARTMEET, THE COFFIN STONE AND TWO RIVERS

DARTMEET IS JUSTIFIABLY ONE OF THE MOST VISITED PLACES ON DARTMOOR. IT IS A FAMOUS BEAUTY SPOT AND IS THE CONFLUENCE OF THE TWO RIVERS, EAST AND WEST DART, THAT GIVE DARTMOOR ITS NAME.

The walk quickly leaves the crowds behind and follows the route of the old Church Way to the Coffin Stone. There was a time when everyone who lived within the ancient Forest of Dartmoor had to go to the church at Lydford for services or for burying their dead. Roads were not suitable for wheeled vehicles and so the body would have to be carried about 12 miles (19km) if the weather was fine or up to 17 miles (27km) if the crossing points of the rivers were impassable. The path to Lydford is known to this day as the Lych Way and can be traced on maps.

In 1260 permission was obtained from the Bishop of Exeter for folk on this side of the moor to go to Widecombe, a mere 6 or 7 miles (10km) away. The path they took became known as the Church Way. Dartmeet Hill is long, and halfway up the bearers of the body would stop for a rest (and possibly some refreshment) at the Coffin Stone. This large block of granite is now split in two and the legend has it that the Almighty took exception to a particularly unpleasant individual being rested there.

Leaving the Coffin Stone the walk continues to Sharp Tor, one of several tors with this name on the moor, passing a very large hut circle on the way. The views over the Dart

Gorge to the south are worth the effort. After crossing Sherberton Common the ancient thatched hamlet of Ponsworthy is reached before walking up the valley of the East Webburn River to another old hamlet known as Jordan.

The route continues alongside the East Webburn, which joins the Dart just a mile or so away, until climbing gently to the edge of Corndon Down. The reward is views right across the moor, this time to the west. The walk then takes us to another ancient farmstead at Sherwell before returning alongside the East Dart to the tearoom at Badger's Holt.

Two rivers, splendid views and a bit of history thrown in!

This is not a difficult walk, but some of the riverside paths are rocky and possibly muddy after rain.

THE BASICS

Distance: 8½ miles / 13.5km

Gradient: Steady climb up from start and one steep descent on lane, otherwise easy gradients

Severity: Moderate / Hard

Time: 4¼ hours

Stiles: One (but beside gate)

Map: OS Explorer OL28 (Dartmoor)

Path description: Moorland and riverside paths and tracks, rocky and possibly muddy in places, quiet lanes and with some open moorland near start

Start point: Dartmeet (GR SX 672733)

Parking: Dartmeet / Badger's Holt car park. Honesty box (PL20 6SG)

Dog friendly: Yes, but on leads on public roads or near animals on the moor

Public toilets: At start

Nearest food: Badger's Holt café at start/finish

Shorter walk near here: Walks For All Ages on Dartmoor - Walks 19 and 20

7 DARTMEET, THE COFFIN STONE AND TWO RIVERS

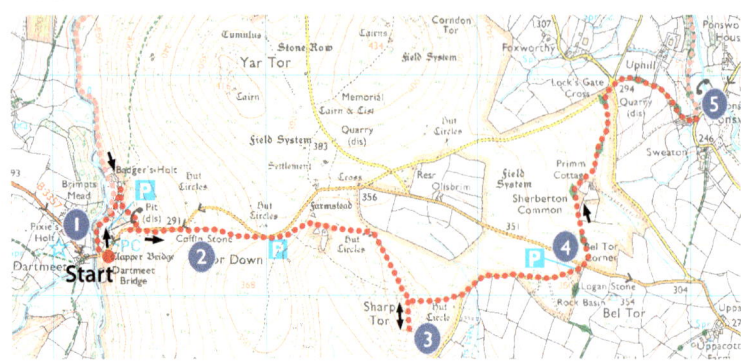

The Route

Before setting out, walk from the parking area alongside the river towards the old clapper bridge and the road bridge built in 1792. Notice the deep grooves in the granite path paving near the honesty box. This was the way blocks of granite were split until relatively recent times.

To see the actual 'Dartmeet', where the East and West Dart rivers join, you will have to cross the road and walk a few metres downstream.

1. From the car park walk away from the bridges to a kissing gate on the right just before signs for Badger's Holt restaurant. Go up the rocky path signed as a public footpath. Turn sharp right by some bird cages and a corrugated iron-roofed farm building towards a bungalow and a broad track.

At the road turn left and walk on the verge for 100m but beware – this is a busy road. When you see a solitary boundary stone inscribed DH by a small layby cross the road and walk up the grassy path inside a slight gully towards a couple of lonely trees. The gully is in fact the sunken track of the old Church Way path before the modern road was built in the 18th century. Continue straight up to the Coffin Stone, about 20m to the right of another tree.

2. Then keep on onwards and upwards alongside the shallow gully passing between two more hawthorn trees. The path meets the road just before a small parking area and ahead is the prominent outline of Sharp Tor.

Twenty metres past the car park bear right on a grassy path towards more hawthorns. Go right after the first tree down a grassy path to pass a large, well-preserved hut circle. Continue down to cross a small stream above the trees of a long-abandoned farm.

After the stream the path veers right through bracken and gorse for a very short distance. Then go immediately left uphill (not straight ahead) to walk through a small group of hawthorn trees and onto a wide grassy path.

The path bears right to head straight towards Sharp Tor. At the tor, climb up through some large boulders and go left of the main summit. Then bear right to the viewpoint over the Dart Gorge. Enjoy the views over the wooded valley and a glimpse of Venford Reservoir below the Holne Moor ridge.

3. Retrace your steps for 100m and then go right down the grassy slope. Head for the corner of the lane and a gate in the stone wall, passing to the left of a solitary tree. Turn left on the lane with field walls on the right and climb up towards Bel Tor.

4. Cross the main road by a parking area and a signpost proclaiming Bel Tor Corner. Head down a grassy path and take the right fork to pass alongside a boundary wall and trees of Primm Cottage with Corndon Tor on the left. Turn right at a lane and then down a steep hill signed Ponsworthy, a hamlet of thatched cottages.

7 DARTMEET, THE COFFIN STONE AND TWO RIVERS

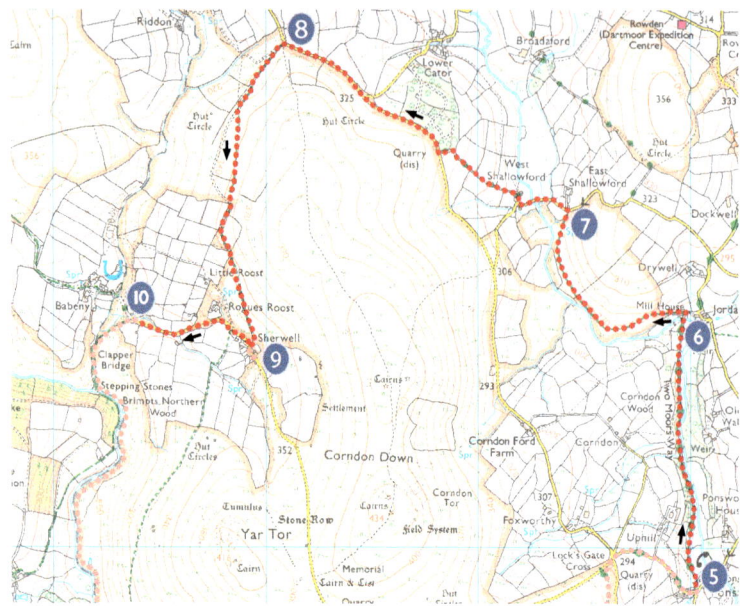

5. Go left just before the ford, known locally as the 'splash', onto a footpath signed to Jordan. This path is rocky and possibly muddy in places as it goes upstream alongside the East Webburn River for ¾ mile (1.2km).

6. Cross a wooden bridge over the river and immediately after the house on the left go sharp left on the footpath signed East Shallowford. (However, if you carry straight on for 50m and take the first turning on the right you will see the magnificent thatched Jordan Manor.)

   Go through a gate and follow the clear path through gorse, in flower most of the year, and with the river now on the left to reach another gate. Again, this path is rocky and muddy in places.

   Soon after the gate, the path veers right up a slope alongside a field wall to reach a lane at East Shallowford.

7. Turn left and go down the lane, crossing a bridge over the river again. Just beyond the bridge go right on a sharp bend. Notice an abandoned apple crusher on the left and go through a metal gate to pass between the farmhouse and farm buildings of West Shallowford. Continue up a green lane and at the top go through a gate and turn right onto a lane. Carry on along this lane for nearly half a mile (750m) and enjoy the views across to Hameldown beyond the Christmas tree plantation. Pass a T-junction and on a right-hand bend bear left on to a sandy track shortly before the lane passes between old walls and gateposts. Note the size of the granite blocks.

8. After 50m on this track bear left, signed as a footpath, onto a grassy path alongside a low bank (the remains of an old field wall) on the right. The path bears left away from this after 400m and heads towards a gate in a stone wall ahead.

    Turn left at the gate and go up the hill alongside the wall on the right as far as the corner. The splendid views to the right include North Hessary Tor (with the communications mast), Bellever Tor, Higher White Tor and the trees of Fernworthy Forest. Further right are Birch Tor and Hookney Tor.

    Go right and after a short distance bear left on a farm track which descends to the hamlet of Sherwell.

9. Go right on the lane but take time to walk a few metres left to look over the gate of Sherwell Farm. This ancient thatched farmhouse is thought to date from the 14th century. The old house on the other side of the road is called Hornet's Castle. Continue on the lane for half a mile (800m), ignoring a side track and footpath signs but passing Rogues Rest and Rogues Roost. The names suggest that this was once a wild and lawless area of the moor!

10. At the bottom of the hill, beside a small passing bay and opposite a metal gate, go left over a tiny clapper bridge. Follow the grassy path beside a stream. Where the path seems to fork, bear right, continuing beside the stream. Pass another, larger, clapper bridge before arriving at an open grassy area by stepping stones over the East Dart River.

    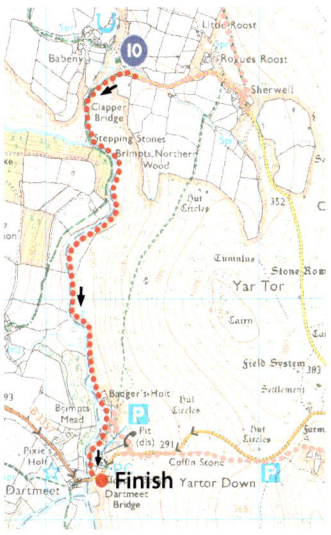

    At the river turn left and follow the River Dart downstream on the riverside path. Take care as this is very rocky and possibly muddy for a short distance before opening out to become a wide grassy path beside the river.

    It is difficult to imagine, in this now restful place, that in the middle of the 19th century there was a tin mine operating on the other side of the river at Brimpts. There is a trail in the woods where some remains can be seen.

    Approaching Badger's Holt the footpath bears left alongside the boundary wall to join the path from which we left the car park but there is a metal gate straight ahead leading to the tearooms. The car park is just beyond.

8 BUCKFAST ABBEY AND HEMBURY WOODS

THIS VARIED WALK STARTS BY GOING THROUGH THE GROUNDS OF BUCKFAST ABBEY AND THEN ALONG A QUIET LANE TO HEMBURY WOODS. HERE WE FOLLOW THE RIVER DART FOR A WHILE BEFORE CLIMBING UP TO HEMBURY FORT.

There was a monastery at Buckfast before the Norman Conquest and the first abbey on the present site was established in 1134. This became one of the wealthiest in the south-west and most of this wealth was from sheep farming and trading in wool, the basis of a woollen industry in the area that lasted until 2013. The monastery, along with all others in England, was dissolved by Henry VIII in 1539 and fell into disrepair.

In 1806 a local merchant purchased the site and built a mansion using stone from the ruins. It is a long story, but in 1882 the site was sold to a group of French Benedictine monks who set out to establish a monastery and rebuild the abbey. Although the abbey church is a mixture of 12th and 13th-century architectural styles it was actually built in the early 20th century and not finished until 1938. The grey local limestone is embellished with a honey-coloured hamstone from Somerset. After the walk, the abbey and grounds are well worth a visit.

Buckfast, and neighbouring Buckfastleigh, were the centre of a prosperous woollen trade in the 19th and 20th centuries and the Higher Mill building, with its impressive waterwheel, can be seen in the grounds of Buckfast Abbey. Water to power the mills was brought by leats (man-made water channels) from high on Dartmoor. The leat for Higher Mill was 4½ miles (7.2km) long and we will cross it twice.

Hembury Woods is full of bluebells in spring and it is a delightful stroll beside the River Dart before climbing up through the woods to reach Hembury Fort. The name Hembury means 'high castle' and it is an appropriate description of the great earthwork on a hilltop. Originally an Iron Age hill fort the site was reused by the Normans centuries later for an earth and timber motte and bailey castle. There is not a great deal to see today but the defensive hilltop position is clear.

Towards the end of the walk we visit Buckfastleigh Church, now a ruin, but perched high on the hilltop and with one of Dartmoor's curiosities in the churchyard.

THE BASICS

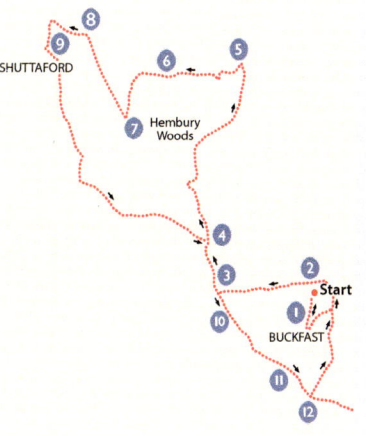

Distance: 9 miles /14.5km
Gradient: Undemanding gradients but several ups and downs. Short section of steps
Severity: Moderate
Time: 4½ hours
Stiles: Two
Map: OS Explorer OL28 (Dartmoor)
Path description: Mostly old tracks and lanes
Start point: Buckfast Abbey
(GR SX 739674)
Parking: Higher Mill Lane, Buckfast (just behind the abbey) or, if you intend to visit the abbey afterwards, in Buckfast Abbey car park (TQ11 0EE)
Dog friendly: Yes, if they can manage the stiles, and on leads on public roads. Not permitted in abbey grounds so start walk at Waypoint 2
Public toilets: Toilets for public use in abbey grounds
Nearest food: Café in abbey grounds
Shorter walk near here: Walks for All Ages on Dartmoor - Walk 20

8 BUCKFAST ABBEY AND HEMBURY WOODS

The Route

1. From your parking place walk to the entrance of the Abbey car park. Go downhill to the mini roundabout and turn left to walk under the arch and into the Abbey grounds. To see the old woollen mill and its impressive waterwheel turn left past the Abbey shop and walk up the path for 50m. Otherwise continue ahead through another archway into Buckfast Road and turn left at the corner.

2. At a road junction go straight on (Grange Road) but notice how the leat bringing water for the mill passes under the road just before the junction. Look left and you will see the mill building and the raised waterway, known as a launder, carrying the water to the top of the waterwheel. Passing a cul-de-sac on the left look out for signs on the gate of one of the houses that it is 'better to be over the hill than under it'.

3. Turn right at the crossroads that is Fritz's Grave. Who Fritz was is not recorded with any certainty and there is more than one possibility. It was, however, common practice in olden times to bury suicides at crossroads to confuse the spirit.

   Shortly afterwards bear right at the fork signed for Hembury Woods. The lane descends to pass the entrance to Hockmoor House where the Higher Mill leat is crossed again.

   The bridge at the bottom crosses the Holy Brook. The name Holy Brook is also another mystery but it seems that it is nothing to do with the fact that it passes through the monastic grounds on its way to join the River Dart.

4. Cross the bridge and take the minor footpath into the woods beside the National Trust sign (not the broader track going left). Keep to the main, but rather narrow, path ignoring side turns to arrive at a parking and picnic area. Cross the road on to a path with an old stone gatepost and walk down into the beech woods, again ignoring side paths.

   Go past a marker post to the Fort but then go right just after a right-hand bend onto another path with a marker post signed to the River. Continue steadily down to reach the riverbank.

   Just beyond this point the riverside path has been eroded and the path has been diverted up some steps on the left. Climb the steps and then descend again to the river.

   Walk along this delightful stretch of the River Dart but beware of tree roots on the path. Cross several small footbridges to arrive at the boundary of the National Trust property at a gate.

8 BUCKFAST ABBEY AND HEMBURY WOODS

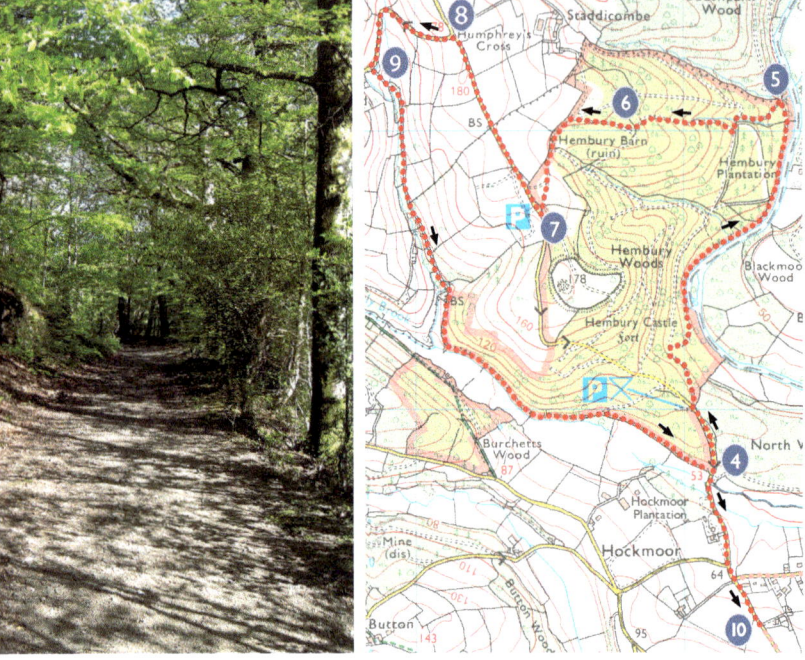

5. Turn sharp left here and up the rocky track (not the path that appears to go up alongside the fence). Follow the path uphill, with a stream alongside, to a T-junction. Go left here, fording the little stream, and almost immediately turn right (almost doubling back) onto another track up into the woods.

   This is the longest uphill stretch but, after a bit of effort, reaches the top where you should go right to reach a gate with a stile beside it. Cross the stile and bear left by the old piles of logs.

6. Go left again at the next junction through a gate beside some fire beaters. Pass the remains of a ruined barn and through another gate with a stile beside it to continue straight on (ignoring two other tracks on the right).

   At a further gate there is an information board about Hembury Fort. Pass through this gate, cross the defensive ditch and bear slightly right to reach the high point of the fort. There is not a lot to see other than this mound and ditch but the views make it obvious why the fort was built on this site.

7. Retrace your steps to the gate with the information board and back to the next gate. Cross the stile on the left to reach a parking area and a lane. At this point go right to walk along the lane with distant views opening up on either side. The high ridge to the left is Holne Moor and it is there that the leat bringing water to power the old mill at Buckfast starts.

8. Turn left just before a wooden barn at Humphrey's Cross (shown on the map but there is no signpost). This lane brings us to the ancient farm of Shuttaford. The listed farmhouse is believed to date from the 16th century.

9. Turn left onto an old green lane immediately before the stone farm buildings but be careful: there is no sign. This path, possibly wet in places, gently descends through the woods beside a stream and, further on, the Holy Brook itself.

   Bear right at a path junction and then right again at a second to arrive at the lane by the bridge over the Holy Brook that we passed earlier. Walk back up the lane as far as Fritz's Grave but now carry straight on up the hill.

10. There is not much traffic on this lane as you pass a side road on the left to arrive at a fork (with a bench on the left). Continue ahead for 200m to reach a crossroads but be careful, as this section of road can be busier, especially in summer months.

11. Go straight ahead at the crossroads signed as a no through road and walk towards the steeple of Buckfastleigh Church, visible over the hedgerows. A church steeple is a rarity on Dartmoor, and indeed the whole of Devon, where most churches only have towers.

    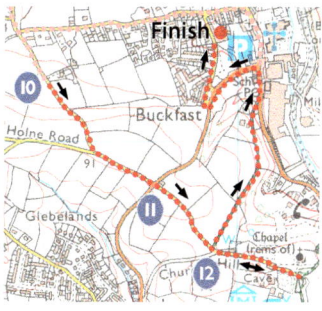

    Bear left at the junction at the top of Church Hill and look out for a footpath sign on the left as this is the return route. However, carry on for another 200m to reach the gate into the churchyard of Buckfastleigh Church. The church is a ruin following an arson attack in 1992 but the substantial slate-roofed building to one side is the tomb of the infamous Squire Richard Cabell. He died in 1677 and was described as a 'monstrously evil man'. In order to make sure that his soul did not escape, a huge slab was placed on top of his grave and the building that you see, complete with iron bars, was constructed. Despite all this, there are all sorts of stories and legends associated with the evil squire. Underneath the church is a whole series of caves which are occasionally open to the public.

12. After looking around the ruins retrace your steps to the top of Church Hill and turn right onto the signed footpath. Cross a field keeping to the hedge on the left and, as you approach the gate at the far side, the tower of Buckfast Abbey becomes visible.

    Go down this ancient path, once the route that parishioners would have had to take to reach the parish church.

    At the road, turn left to the Abbey and the cars. The last woollen mill in the area, which closed in 2013, was situated here.

9 HARFORD AND WESTERN BEACON

Another very varied walk with a delightful river, wild open moorland, a quiet stone-lined country lane and plenty of history. Starting alongside the River Erme the walk takes us to Harford Moor and Western Beacon, one of the southernmost high points of Dartmoor.

The walk starts close to the centre of Ivybridge, a town which owes its existence to the River Erme. The ancient Ivy Bridge, recorded as long ago as 1292, was one of the packhorse crossings of the river and was later widened to accommodate wheeled traffic. In the industrial age, the waters of the river powered a number of corn and paper mills and the last paper mill closed only a few years ago.

The beginning of the walk is alongside what must be one of the most charming stretches of river close to a town centre anywhere in the country. The Erme is a joy at any time of the year as it cascades through a wooded valley and over a jumble of little waterfalls.

Leaving the river behind there is a climb up to Hanger Down, a wide open space above the town. There are views here in all directions towards the sea, the moor and the South Devon countryside. The walk continues along an ancient lane with moss-covered stone walls to a 16th-century bridge over the River Erme and the hamlet of Harford. Time has passed this place by and only a few people live here now but the typical Dartmoor church is as fine a place as any to pause awhile.

A lane leads us up onto Harford Moor where we walk beside some of the stones of the second-longest prehistoric stone row on Dartmoor, in total about 1¼ miles (2km) long.

The Redlake Tramway is much more recent. It was said that it commenced on the edge of nowhere and ended in the middle of nowhere. The narrow-gauge tramway was built to serve the china clay pits at Red Lake and was about 7½ miles (12km) long. Looking at the Dartmoor scene today it is difficult to imagine that this enterprise employed up to a hundred men in the early 20th century. The tramway transported the workers and supplies whilst the clay was piped by gravity to the drying plant, the site of which we will see from Western Beacon. To this day the track is known locally as the "Buffing Billy".

From the Beacon another old drovers' path brings us back to Ivybridge.

THE BASICS

Distance: 10 miles / 16km

Gradient: Easy gradients but with one moderately steep descent

Severity: Moderate / Hard

Time: 4½ hours

Stiles: None

Map: OS Explorer OL28 (Dartmoor)

Path description: Riverside and moorland tracks and some open moorland. Should not be attempted in poor visibility without good navigation skills. Short distance on a quiet lane

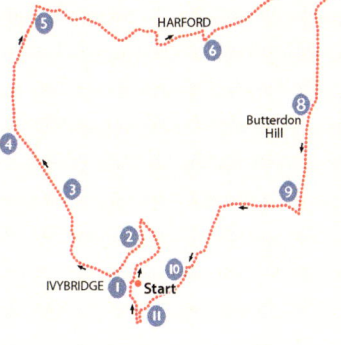

Start point: Station Road, Ivybridge, near viaduct (GR SX 635569)

Parking: Roadside in Station Road, near viaduct (PL21 0AH)

Dog friendly: Yes, but on leads if near animals on the moor or on public road

Public toilets: None on walk. Available in Ivybridge town centre

Nearest food: Several cafés and pubs in Ivybridge

Shorter walk near here: Walks for All Ages on Dartmoor - Walk 18

9 HARFORD AND WESTERN BEACON

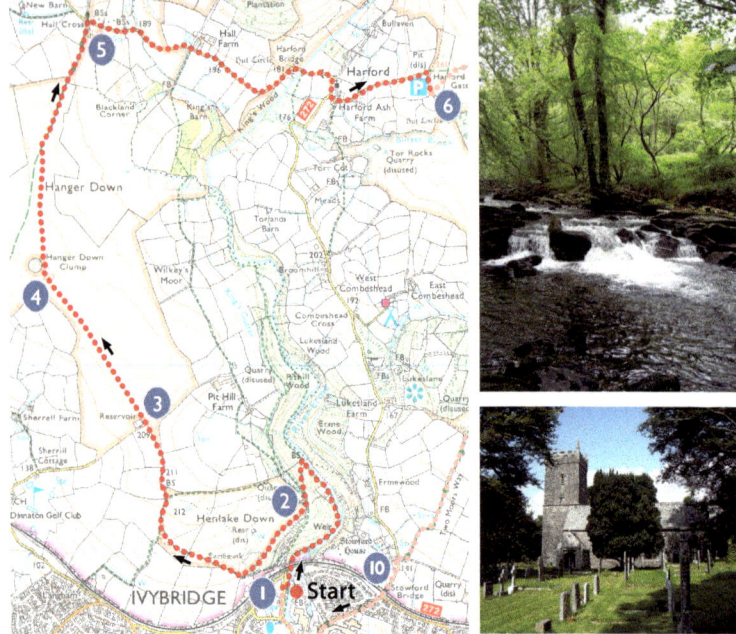

The Route

1. Take the public footpath through a metal gate and under the viaduct. The viaduct was built in the 1890s, but the piers of the original Brunel viaduct of 1842 still stand beside the newer one. Walk up this delightful woodland path alongside the River Erme as it tumbles down over a series of small waterfalls. Pass a small disused open-air swimming pool on the left and shortly afterwards go sharp left uphill on a signed footpath just before a picnic area. The path climbs fairly steeply to meet a lane.

2. Go right and immediately left through a metal gate. Take the path running alongside the old stone wall through beech woods. Soon after passing a small reservoir there is a path junction just above a gate. Turn right and climb on a well-trodden path, possibly muddy, through gorse and bracken. Views soon open up ahead over the town of Ivybridge and towards the sea in Plymouth Sound. Go straight on at a path junction and then bear left to a pair of gates. Pause at the metal gate to admire the view and then go through the wooden gate and up an old green lane with stone walls on either side.

3. Go through a metal gate and continue alongside the stone wall. When the wall ends continue forward in the same direction onto Hanger Down with a plantation of trees ahead. Originally called the Round Plantation they are now simply the Hanger Down Clump. The 360-degree views are again towards Plymouth and the

sea, the huge china clay workings at Lee Moor, and the moorland skyline from Shell Top to Western Beacon across the valleys of the Rivers Erme and Yealm.

4. Turn right at the trees and walk across the open moorland heading almost due north slightly right of a line of trees to a gate in the corner. There is no clear path, and the bridleway is not waymarked as well as it could be although there are a number of blue-topped wooden posts. Keep parallel with a post-and-wire fence on the right and before long a track leading to the gate becomes clear. Go through the gate, signed as a bridleway, and continue on this old drovers' path as far as Hall Cross.

5. Turn right on the lane and, after a short distance, pass Hall Farm on the left, parts of which date from the 17th and 18th centuries. After nearly half a mile (650m) cross Harford Bridge, the only bridge over the River Erme above Ivybridge. There is a short, sharp uphill stretch before reaching Harford Church. This is a rather typical and plain Dartmoor church but, nevertheless, worth visiting. In the churchyard is an old wayside cross removed from its original position at the road junction. Turn left up the hill signed to Harford Moor.

9 HARFORD AND WESTERN BEACON

6. Go through the gate beside the cattle grid, right past a small parking area and immediately left up a wide grassy path away from the field boundary wall. There are some conifer trees on the right around a small reservoir. Hangershell Rock soon appears ahead and although not on the crest of the hill it is an obvious landmark. It may only be a small tor but it is a very good example of how the joints of granite weather into what looks like a series of blocks.

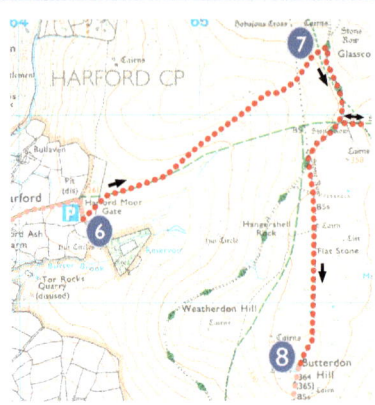

After 1 km (just over half a mile) the path becomes less distinct and skirts to the right around some low-growing gorse clumps. Continue ahead and about 350m further on the path crosses a stone row. This stone row is notable as it is the second longest on Dartmoor although many of the stones are fallen. Look for the line of them to the left towards the top of Piles Hill and to the right towards Butterdon Hill. The path now disappears but continue forward in the same direction over rough grassy moorland for 150m to reach a very substantial track. This is the line of the old Redlake Tramway which was built to transport men and supplies to the china clay works at Red Lake, nearly 6 miles (10km) further into the moor, and was in use from 1910 until its demise in 1932.

7. Turn right and walk down the track for about ¼ mile (400m) and turn left on grassy moorland for another 150m to reach Spurrell's Cross. This ancient wayside cross was on the route from Plympton to South Brent. The village of South Brent can be seen below and the prominent tor to the right is Ugborough Beacon.

Retrace your steps to the tramway and turn left. The track passes through a shallow cutting and as it bends to the left you will see the stone row again. Leave the tramway to walk up alongside the stone row. There is a substantial cairn on the left and the rock on the right is Hangershell Rock, which we saw from a distance earlier. Continue along the stone row to reach two massive cairns and a trig point on the top of Butterdon Hill. The views from this high point (365m or 1,197ft) are splendid, with much of South Devon spread out below.

8. Continue onwards in the same direction, still following a row of stones marking the boundaries of Harford and Ugborough parishes to pass the Longstone and a rather muddy pool known as Black Pool. Pass a single cairn and then the last of the upright stones (the large inscribed H for Harford is clearly visible) to go between two more cairns on Western Beacon. The mound of spoil is from an old quarry just below the summit and there is a good view over Ivybridge. The factory buildings below, with the tall brick chimney, were the drying sheds for the clay from the Red Lake pits.

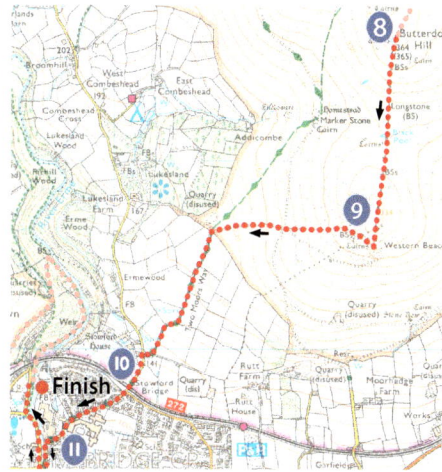

9. Take a minor grassy path back from the quarry edge in the direction of the china clay tips on the horizon and Harford Moor Clump that we passed early on. This path soon becomes wide and straight as it descends to cross a tramway siding to the quarry and then the Redlake Tramway itself. Continue downhill to a gate and go left into a drovers' lane, signed as a bridleway. Walk down this rather rocky track to meet a lane opposite Stowford House. The core of the house very old but it was extensively modernised in the 18th century by the then owner of the old paper mill that we will pass shortly.

10. Turn left, and after a few metres cross over a railway bridge carrying the main Penzance to London Paddington railway. At the crossroads carry straight on down Harford Road. This passes the community college on the left and then some old industrial buildings on the right. For over 200 years this was a paper mill that produced high-quality papers until it closed in 2013.

11. At the ancient Ivy Bridge turn right to cross the river, noticing old parish boundary stones built into the parapet. Go immediately right again into Station Road and just around the next corner you will see the viaduct again.

10 ROBOROUGH DOWN AND SHAUGH BRIDGE

An easy walk across Roborough Down before descending into the wooded valley where the Rivers Meavy and Plym meet. We follow the River Meavy upstream before returning along the route of a horse-drawn tramway, built nearly 200 years ago.

Starting near Clearbrook, the walk follows the old water channel, now dry, known as the Plymouth Leat. This 17-mile (27km) long leat was dug in the winter of 1590/1 and was Plymouth's principal water supply, bringing water from Dartmoor until the turn of the 20th century, when Burrator Reservoir was built. What we see today has been upgraded and improved over the years, but is still on the original route and we can but marvel at the engineering skills of 400 years ago.

At the end of the stroll over the Down we walk along a quiet lane to reach an old railway line, now a trail for walkers and cyclists. The line followed the valley of the River Plym from Plymouth to this point and then went on to Yelverton and Tavistock, with a branch to Princetown. The old station platform still survives but there have been no trains since 1962.

Shaugh Bridge is where the Rivers Meavy and Plym merge. This picturesque spot is a joy at any time of year, as the rivers tumble over the boulders through the oak woodland. The path then takes us on an old tramway around the side of the Dewerstone. The Dewerstone is a fine rock face, a favourite with climbers, that towers above the River Plym and was once the site of an Iron Age fort. Legend has it that the Dewerstone is the haunt of Dewer, otherwise known as Satan, who hunts with a phantom pack of black hounds.

We then walk up the valley of the River Meavy, passing the remains of old quarry workings and tin-mining activities. The return is along a level path, the track of the Plymouth and Dartmoor horse-drawn railway which ran from Plymouth to Princetown, a distance of 25½ miles (41km). It was opened in 1823 and was built to an unusual gauge, 4 ft 6 in, which became known as the Dartmoor gauge. We will be able to see the granite setts onto which the rails were fixed and the building in which the horses were stabled before meeting the Plymouth Leat once again.

BRADWELL'S LONGER WALKS

THE BASICS

Distance: 9 miles / 14.5km or 6 miles / 9.5km

Gradient: Easy gradients but one moderately steep descent on a lane

Severity: Moderate

Time: 4¼ hours or 2¾ hours

Stiles: Five

Map: OS Explorer OL28 (Dartmoor)

Path description: Good footpaths, tracks (including a short disused railway tunnel) and minor lanes

Start point: Leat Bridge, Clearbrook (GR SX 519651)

Parking: Car parking area by bridge over old leat on the edge of Clearbrook village (near PL20 6JD)

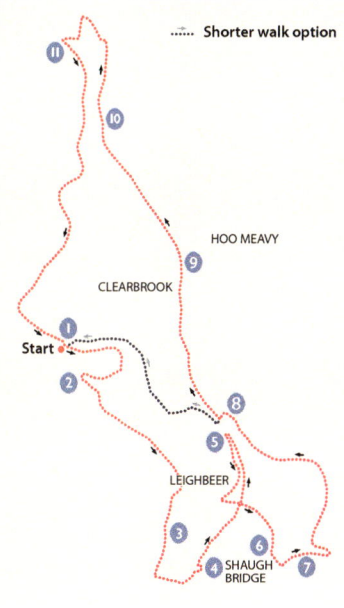

Dog friendly: Yes, if they can manage the stile and on leads if near animals on the moor or on public road

Public toilets: None

Nearest food: Skylark Inn, Clearbrook

10 ROBOROUGH DOWN AND SHAUGH BRIDGE

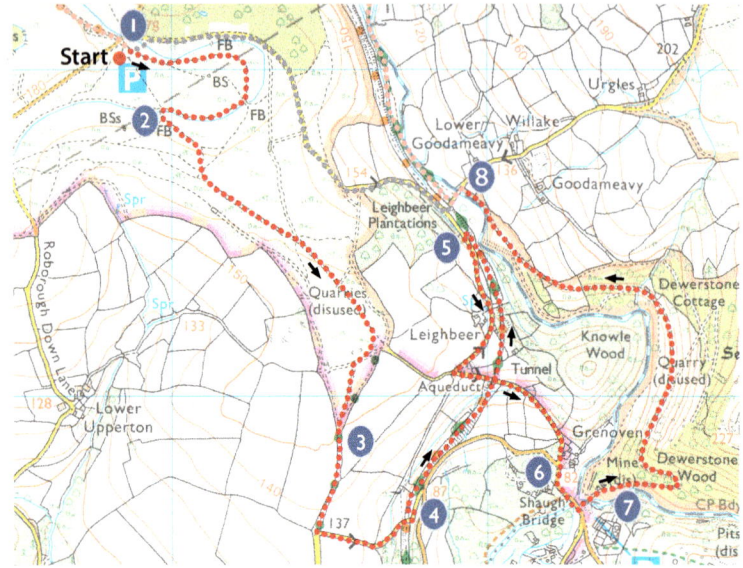

The Route

1. Walk away from the car park with the Plymouth Leat, now granite lined but dry, and Clearbrook village on the left. There are good views across the wooded valley to Sheeps Tor and, further away, the communications mast on North Hessary Tor. Pass a bridge over the leat and then, after going round a fairly sharp bend, a second bridge.

2. After a further 300m, turn left over a third, much wider, concrete bridge. Walk down the grassy track that bears slightly left with gorse bushes on either side. After 150m fork right towards the church tower in the distance and pass a concrete water trough. Ignore side paths as the track bends to the left and then heads straight across the down. There are several tracks here, but keep to the main central one, passing a holly tree and walking towards a hedge boundary and trees to the left.

   Cross a track and continue onward in the same direction. When nearing the field walls, bear round to the right on the grassy moorland although there are no clear paths to follow here. Pass a small parking area and a lane and continue alongside a field wall on the left. About 250m after the parking area there is a gate in the corner of the open moorland.

3. Go through the gate and down a wide green lane to a junction with a minor road. Turn left and the village and church of Shaugh Prior can be seen across the valley. Go down the hill and cross an old railway bridge which is over the platform of what was a station known as Shaugh Bridge Halt on the Plymouth to Tavistock railway. The River Plym can be heard through the trees but not seen.

4. Almost immediately after the bridge go left onto the old platform and then right to walk up the old railway track. Although this is a multi-use trail it is normally quiet and you are not likely to see many cyclists, but take care and look out for them. After about ¼ mile (400m) the track goes through the short Leighbeer Tunnel. It is on a slight curve but there are lights and it is well surfaced.

5. Soon after leaving the tunnel you will see the River Meavy on the right and a gate on the left onto a lane. Go through the gate and turn sharp left to walk uphill. Pass the buildings of Leighbeer Farm and then turn left at a T-junction. Go down this fairly steep hill, which passes over the tunnel through which we have just walked, to reach another junction. Turn left onto this road, signed to Shaugh Prior. Be careful as this is a fairly busy road and there is a sharp corner.

6. It is a very short distance to the bridge over the river at the point where the Meavy and Plym meet. Cross the bridge and immediately go left through a gap in the wall before reaching the parking area. Then go left over a modern footbridge crossing the River Plym and bear right alongside a low wooden barrier. It is difficult to appreciate today but this small area between the two rivers was once a hive of activity. There was an iron ore mine and a brickworks opposite the bridge that  we have just crossed and there are still ruins to be seen among the trees. There were also clay drying kilns where the car park now is, the clay being piped down from the pits at Lee Moor.

7. Go up the moderately steep incline paved with blocks of granite and go sharp left near the top (not continuing on the minor path ahead). The track levels out onto an old tramway. The evenly spaced granite blocks to which the rails were fixed are clearly visible. Pass two small quarries on the right and then bear left at a fork. This is the bottom of an inclined plane up to some more old quarry workings where trucks were hauled up the slope by a cable arrangement.

Pass Dewerstone Cottage, once the quarry office but now an outdoor adventure centre. Ignore the left fork just beyond the building and go through a gate and a cutting and then over an embankment. Bear right on the track but notice the bridge on the left that was a planned link from the tramway to the GWR branch line over the river but was never completed.

10 ROBOROUGH DOWN AND SHAUGH BRIDGE

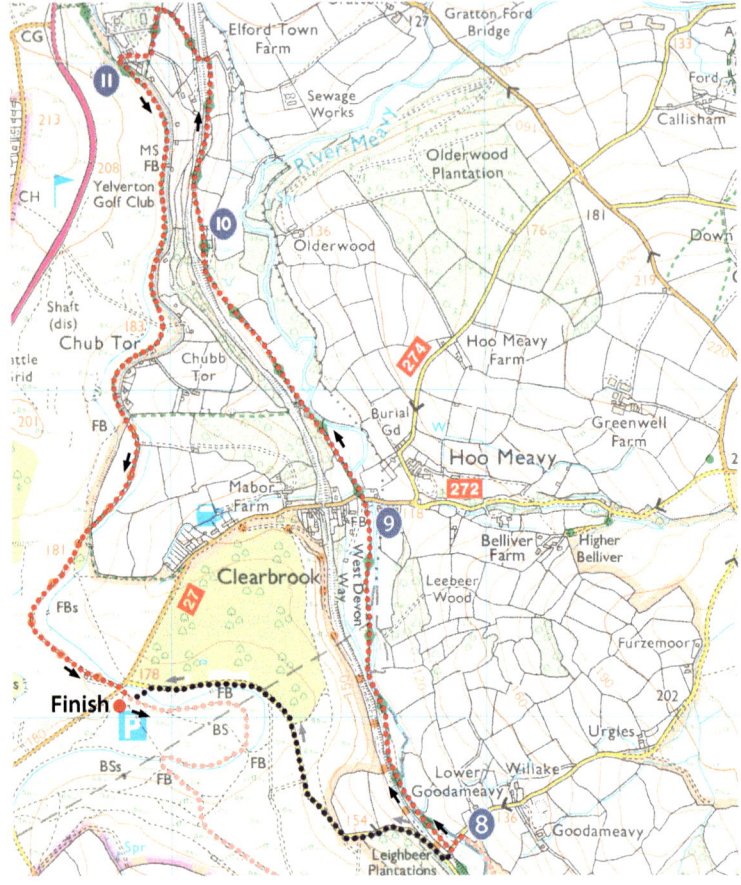

8. Go over a stile at Goodameavy Bridge and turn left to cross the river.

   To shorten the walk at this point go under the old railway bridge, turn right and walk up the hill on the lane and back to the car park.

   Otherwise, immediately go right over a second stile just before the railway bridge onto a footpath signed for Clearbrook. Follow the path, which may be muddy after rain, across the meadow with the River Meavy now on the right. Go over another stile and for a short distance the path is high above the river alongside the course of an old leat which supplied water to a copper mine about two miles away.

   Go over a fourth stile and into the riverside meadow. Go through a gate into a second meadow leading to Hoo Meavy bridge with a ladder stile beside it onto a lane.

9. Continue straight on (not over the bridge) and onto a public footpath signed to Yelverton. There are remains of mining activity all the way along this track. Water can be seen draining from old workings and there are ruined buildings in the

woodland. Yeoland Consols was a tin mine active in the second half of the 19th century and some of the stone buildings now in domestic use alongside the track date from this time.

10. Go through a gate and up the public footpath beside the entrance to Yeoland House. The path climbs up through oak woodland and then alongside the old railway line with a post-and-wire fence on the right. There are good views across the field and the river valley towards Sheeps Tor.

   Go through a metal gate at the end, turn left under the old railway bridge and immediately right. Then turn left at the next junction and up to a wooden gate.

11. Cross the Plymouth Leat and bear right to meet the old Plymouth and Dartmoor horse-drawn railway. Go sharp left, signed Clearbrook, to walk down the track of the old tramway, now tarmac, with another old leat on the right. Just past the entrance to a house called Roughways, notice a milestone indicating that it is 13 miles to the terminus of the tramway on the estuary of the River Plym.

   Go through a double gate, after which is a good section of the old tramway granite blocks onto which the rails were fixed, to reach another pair of gates. Continue ahead on the cycle path with the old tramway now on the right and the Plymouth Leat on the left. Pass another milestone (12) and then an old stone building, which was originally built as stables for the tramway horses, and back to the parking area.

11 BURRATOR RESERVOIR AND SHEEPS TOR

THIS IS NOT JUST A WATERSIDE RAMBLE AROUND A RESERVOIR. USING THE TRACK OF A LONG-DISUSED RAILWAY THE WALK TAKES US INTO OPEN MOORLAND BEFORE ENTERING MIXED WOODLAND AND THEN UP TO THE HEIGHTS OF SHEEPS TOR.

For 300 years Plymouth's principal water supply had been an open leat, bringing the waters of the River Meavy 17 miles (27km) across the southern edge of Dartmoor but by the late 19th century this was proving inadequate. Plymouth's population was growing, as was the demand for water by industry. A severe winter when the leat became blocked was the final straw and a decision was taken to build a reservoir. The dam was completed in 1898 and raised by 10 feet in the 1920s. The reservoir's appearance today is more like a Swiss lake surrounded, as it is, by mixed woodland and the craggy heights of Leather Tor and Sheeps Tor.

The early part of the walk is along the track of the Princetown branch railway, which closed in 1956. Originally this had been a horse-drawn tramway, built by the Plymouth and Dartmoor Railway, which opened in 1823 to bring stone from quarries near Princetown and to serve the prison town.

There are good views of the reservoir and before long the Devonport Leat is encountered. Before 1914 Plymouth and Devonport were separate towns and Devonport had constructed a leat for its own water supply. This was built in the 1790s and was 28 miles (45km) long. It starts from much higher on the moor, almost 1,400 feet (425m) above sea level. From Burrator onwards the routes of the Plymouth and Devonport leats are very close to each other. We will walk alongside another section later in the walk.

The railway leaves the reservoir behind and open moorland views begin as the track sweeps in gentle curves. In the distance can be seen the hills of Bodmin Moor whilst closer to hand, across the valley of the River Walkham, is a skyline dominated by a line of 1,500-foot (450m) tors.

Later we pass several ruined farms which were abandoned due to fears that farming activities were polluting the reservoir water supply. Evidence of both medieval and 19th-century tin production in the area can also be seen.

Just a short diversion from our route up to Sheeps Tor are the Yellowmead stone circles. These are most unusual being four circles, one within the other.

BRADWELL'S LONGER WALKS

THE BASICS

Distance: 10½ miles / 17km or 7½ miles / 12km

Gradient: Mostly easy going but one short steep up and one short steep down on the longer option

Severity: Moderate but shorter option easier

Time: 5 hours or 3½ hours

Stiles: Two

Map: OS Explorer OL28 (Dartmoor)

Path description: Good tracks and old railway line with some open moor on longer walk. Possibly muddy in places.

Start point: Burrator Dam (GR SX 551680)

Parking: Roadside close to dam (PL20 6PE)

Dog friendly: Yes, if they can manage stiles, but on leads if near animals on the moor or on public road

Public toilets: At Burrator Lodge, 250m from start

Nearest food: Burrator Inn at Dousland or Royal Oak at Meavy, both 1 mile (1.5km) from the start

67

11 BURRATOR RESERVOIR AND SHEEPS TOR

The Route

1. Walk along the road away from the dam with the reservoir on the right for 200m. Just before the waterfall turn sharp left up the stony track signed as a cycle path.

    Go sharp right at the top onto the track bed of the old railway. Across the valley is Sheeps Tor and Sheepstor church tower can be seen above the trees. There is a good view of the reservoir as you pass the rusting remains of Burrator Halt, a popular destination for day trippers 60 or 70 years ago.

2. Go through a gate and, just beyond, water can be seen gushing from a pipe as a waterfall and into the reservoir. The Devonport Leat still carries water from high on Dartmoor but from this point it is piped to a treatment works whilst the overflow empties into the reservoir. Although no longer carrying water, the route of the leat can still be traced for many more miles across the moor.

    Go through a second gate, and cross the road on a modern footbridge where the leat can be seen curving away along the hillside.

3. Cross another lane where there was once a level crossing and soon views of Kit Hill, Caradon Hill and Bodmin Moor open up ahead. Go over the Princetown road on a very impressive bridge erected in 2015 and through a number of gates into open countryside. Soon the fields give way to open moorland on both sides and as the track curves a line of tors dominates the skyline, the higher ones being Great Staple Tor and Great Mis Tor.

4. About 100m before reaching a line of fence posts on the left and with King Tor ahead go sharp right up a wide track. Continue as far as a car park and cross the Princetown road. Although the path is not as obvious beyond here, continue walking in the same direction towards the corner of the conifer plantation, then bear slightly left to walk along with the wall on the right. Look out for a cist (a Bronze Age burial chamber) just off the path on the left.

    Go through the gateway in the corn ditch wall. Walls of this type are probably of medieval origin as they were designed to keep deer out. Walk down the old fields to the ruins of Stanlake Farm.

5. Cross the Devonport Leat, go through a gate and continue on the path alongside the water for almost half a mile (600m) to arrive at a path junction.

    At this point there is an option to shorten the walk by continuing alongside the leat. Follow the track down to a lane and continue forward with the leat now on the left. Stay on the lane past an old, but reroofed, stone barn before going uphill with a conifer woodland on the right. When the leat crosses the road yet again go left on the footpath alongside the water. Cross a lane and

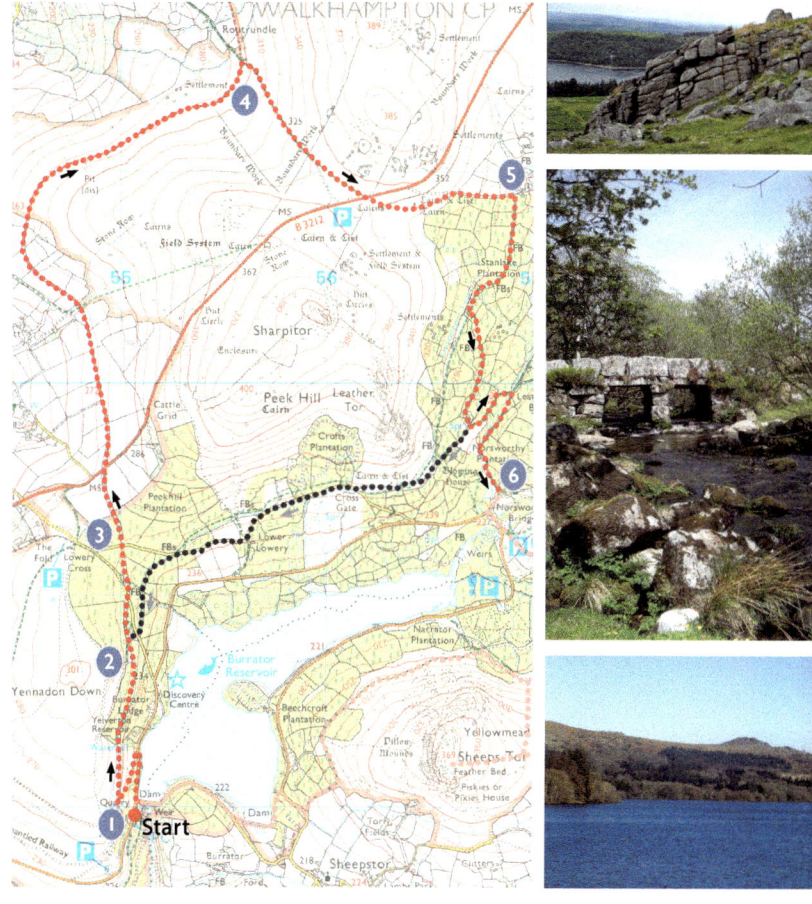

continue walking alongside the leat until reaching the point where we saw the water disappearing at Waypoint 2. Walk back to the cars along the old railway, the way you came.

Otherwise turn left, signed as a footpath to Leather Tor Farm. Go down this good track with Down Tor immediately ahead. Cross a stile beside a gate by the ruins of Leather Tor Farm (there is a historical information board on the right) and turn left.

Pass a potato cave, a cool and dark place where the farmers would have stored root crops, to arrive at Leather Tor bridge over the River Meavy. Turn right to walk alongside the river but after about 300m look out for a stile in the wire fence on the right with a white-topped marker just inside. Down on the riverbank is the remains of a medieval tinner's blowing house with several mould stones visible.

11 BURRATOR RESERVOIR AND SHEEPS TOR

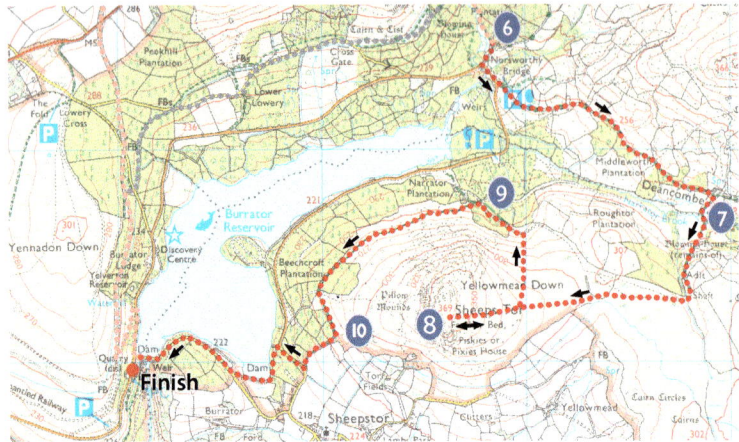

6. Go right at a path junction and then left at the road with a bridge both to the right and left. This is where the River Meavy and a small stream known as the Newleycombe Lake join to empty into Burrator Reservoir.

   Just beyond the bridge bear left by a parking area up a rocky lane (ignoring a footpath on the left). Continue along this ancient trackway, passing the ruins of Middleworth Farm to arrive at the ruins of yet another farm, known as Deancombe. Just before the ruined buildings turn right on a bridleway signed to Sheepstor Common.

7. Cross the Narrator Brook on a small clapper bridge and follow the path around to the right, still signed for Sheepstor Common. Ignore a stile on the right but notice the good views of Leather Tor beyond and Down Tor behind.

   The path from here up to a gate at the top is moderately steep and has been eroded by the Dartmoor rain and so care is needed. Go through the gate and bear right to cross the stream and continue up the rocky track ahead. Bear slightly right to avoid a gorse thicket and cross a low bank, probably the route of an old leat, by a PCWW (Plymouth Corporation Water Works) marker post. There are a number of these to be seen and they mark the extent of the catchment area for the reservoir. Head for the grassy track towards the left side of the summit of Sheeps Tor ahead, passing another PCWW post on the way. Look to your left and you will see Yellowmead circles in the direction of Gutter Tor.

8. Pause to admire the view on Sheeps Tor. Immediately below is Sheepstor Church and in the distance can be seen Plymouth and the sea in Plymouth Sound. Further to the right, over the reservoir, are the hills of Bodmin Moor.

   The descent from Sheeps Tor is not for the faint-hearted and an easier route is to retrace your steps on the grassy path for about 300m to the last PCWW post that we went past. Turn left to walk due north across the grassy open moor towards the mast on North Hessary Tor. Then take the grassy path to your left downhill, quite steeply towards a gateway in a stone wall ahead.

9. Go left through the gate and walk down the stony track to a path junction by two large gates. Go left on the track (not over the stile) and continue straight on where the path forks, signed as a bridlepath to Sheepstor Village.

   This path follows the contour around the base of Sheeps Tor and may be muddy in places. After a short distance between walls the path opens out again before following a stone wall to reach a gate.

10. Go through the gate and down an old packhorse track known as Joey's Lane. Turn right at the bottom onto a tarmac lane but after just 150m go left through a gate onto the reservoir perimeter path. This takes us over an earth embankment, which is a secondary dam to hold back the waters of the reservoir, to another gate. Go through this and walk along the road and over the top of Burrator Dam back to the start.

12 RINGMOOR DOWN AND DRIZZLECOMBE

An easy walk on the southern side of Dartmoor with great views, two Bronze Age stone rows, an excellent stone circle and historic remains of old industries. The upper reaches of the River Plym make this a most interesting walk.

Much of Dartmoor's character and history is due to granite. Most of Dartmoor is on granite and the distinctive tors that are a unique feature of the landscape are the result of weathering of this rock. China clay is also the result of weathering and the decomposition of the granite mass. China clay quarrying has been a big industry on parts of Dartmoor for nearly 200 years. Much older is tin mining. Minerals were deposited in the joints and fractures of the granite, some of which contain valuable metal ores such as tin and copper. There is a long history of extracting these minerals, but mostly tin, on Dartmoor. The earliest form was streaming the alluvial deposits in river beds. Then came surface mining and later deep-shaft mining. Workers in this inhospitable landscape had to be fed and this gave rise to yet another industry – warrening for the rearing of rabbits. We will see all of these on the walk.

Commercial rabbit warrens were an important industry until as late as the 1950s and Ditsworthy was one of the largest on Dartmoor, covering an area of several hundred acres. The rabbits lived in long cigar-shaped structures built of stone and covered with earth into which the rabbits could burrow. These are known as pillow mounds and are marked on the map. The rabbits were flushed out by dogs and ferrets kept by the warrener at the warren house.

The area is rich in Bronze Age remains and the walk visits the Brisworthy stone circle on one side of Legis Tor and the Drizzlecombe stone rows on the other. One of the standing stones is said to be the tallest on Dartmoor and nearby is a burial cairn known as the Giant's Basin and three prehistoric hut circle settlements.

From Higher Hartor Tor the route is down the old miners' track past part of Eylesbarrow tin mine where there are the remains of some buildings and former ore-smelting mills to be seen. An easy climb up to Gutter Tor takes us to Ringmoor Down and then a level stroll with splendid views brings us back to the car.

THE BASICS

Distance: 8 miles / 12.5km
Gradient: Easy gradients
Severity: Leisurely
Time: 3½ hours
Stiles: Four
Map: OS Explorer OL28 (Dartmoor)
Path description: Paths on open moorland or stony tracks with some small stream crossings. Should not be attempted in poor visibility without good navigation skills
Start point: Ringmoor Cottage (GR SX 558666)
Parking: Small parking area by cattle grid at Ringmoor Cottage (PL20 6PQ)
Dog friendly: Yes, if they can manage stiles, but on leads if near animals on the moor
Public toilets: None
Nearest food: Royal Oak, Meavy or cafés at Yelverton
Shorter walk near here: Walks for All Ages on Dartmoor - Walk 17

12 RINGMOOR DOWN AND DRIZZLECOMBE

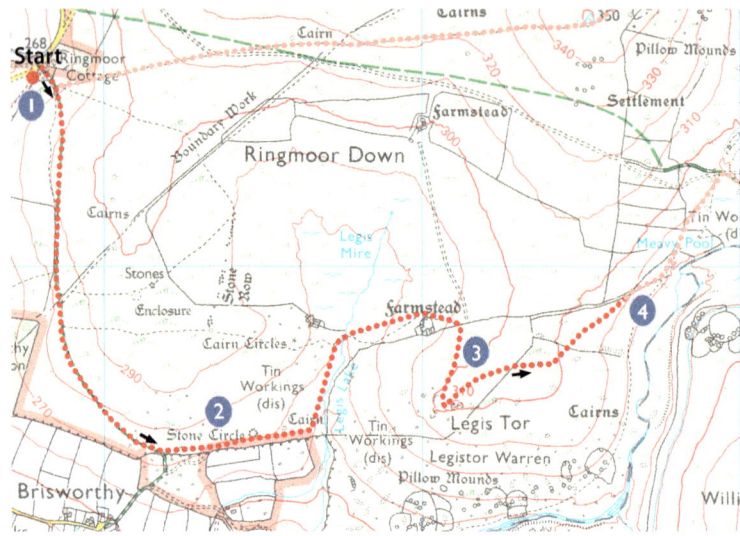

The Route

1. Go over the stile at the back of the parking area signed as a public footpath to Brisworthy. Take the grassy track ahead which veers to the right away from Ringmoor Cottage. Bear slightly left at a path crossing as the track climbs gently. It follows an old boundary wall towards a copse for a while but when the wall turns towards the copse keep straight ahead. Ignore several path crossings and head towards the flat-topped spoil heap from the clay works visible on the horizon.

China clay production at Lee Moor started as long ago as 1830 and at one time the quarry was one of the largest man-made holes in the ground anywhere in the world. Although the spoil heaps are something of an eyesore, big efforts are now being made to minimise the environmental impact.

The path bends around to the left as it nears a field wall and a post-and-wire fence. Continue alongside this wall and fence with Legis Tor ahead to reach the Brisworthy stone circle. This is a splendid example of a Bronze Age stone circle. Some restoration work was carried out about 100 years ago and stones which had fallen were re-erected.

2. From the circle continue alongside the wall and fence towards Legis Tor. Just before reaching a stream, which goes by the name of Legis Lake, go left by the holly tree to walk above the old tinners' stream workings. The disturbed ground is the result of exploration for tin many centuries ago with spoil heaps of discarded waste from the alluvial streaming.

   Turn right to cross the stream on stepping stones and up the stony track. This bears away from the wall on the right as it climbs gently uphill before swinging towards a gate. Go through this and across the moor to reach Legis Tor.

   On the southern side of the tor, i.e. the far side, is an almost complete vermin trap but it may be hidden in the bracken in summer. The rabbits which were bred in the warrens had many predators and there are quite a number of vermin traps in the area designed to catch stoats and weasels and other small creatures.

3. To continue the walk go left at the tor towards a stile beside a gate. Cross the stile, and go left on a faint track away from the fence and towards the clump of trees around Ditsworthy Warren House in the distance. There are a number of pillow mounds on both sides of the path but the best examples are to be seen closer to the warren house. Cross an old wall and bear right on a much better grassy path towards the River Plym in the valley below. Across the river on the hillside can be seen the horizontal line of a leat which, at one time, provided water power to a tin and copper mine known as Bottle Hill Mine and later to the Lee Moor china clay works in the distance.

4. Bear left at a fork to reach a pair of gates. Go through these and carry straight on to reach a stony track. Turn right to pass the substantial waste tips from tin workings and more pillow mounds as the track approaches the warren house. If the house looks familiar this may be because it appeared as the family home in Steven Spielberg's film of **War Horse**.

   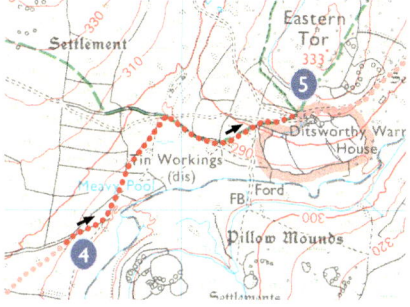

   The warren house is several hundred years old but the ruin adjoining with the slit windows may be even older, possibly dating from the 15th century.

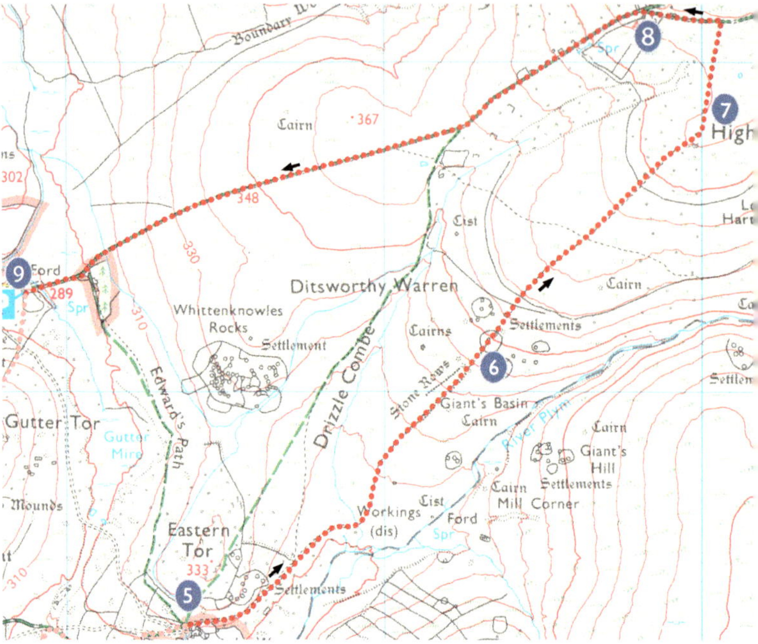

12 RINGMOOR DOWN AND DRIZZLECOMBE

5. Take the track behind the house but notice the wall enclosure on the right. This was a pound where the dogs which were used to flush the rabbits out of the pillow mounds were kept and you can see several kennels built into the wall.

The track crosses a small stream and then a wider one with stepping stones (although it is possible to jump across a little higher up). Go slightly left on the grassy path towards the huge standing stones ahead. As you walk up the stone row the Giant's Basin is on the right and a second, smaller, stone row is on the left. The two stone rows are almost parallel and the path passes between the two cairns, one at the end of each stone row, and on towards the prehistoric settlements further up the hillside.

6. Continue uphill to go through the broken-down walls of one of the Bronze Age settlements with several hut circles on either side. Carry on to reach Higher Hartor Tor. The views from here are magnificent with Plymouth Sound, the city of Plymouth and the Cornish hills on Bodmin Moor spread out in the distance. Closer at hand is Sheeps Tor, and on the other side of Burrator Reservoir (which is just out of view), Leather Tor and Sharpitor.

7. From Higher Hartor Tor, take the grassy path half left towards Eylesbarrow and another stony track. This track leads to Plym Ford where an ancient path, now known as the Abbots Way, crossed the river on the route from the abbeys at Buckfast and Tavistock. However, turn left away from the river and pass the ruins of several old mine buildings on the right and wall field enclosures on the left.

8. Go left at a fork to walk downhill past the ruins of more old buildings and mine shafts. On the right is a striking skyline of Dartmoor tors including Great Links Tor and Great Mis Tor and the communications mast on North Hessary Tor. Pass several marker stones inscribed PCWW 1917 denoting the catchment area of Burrator Reservoir, built by Plymouth Corporation Water Works some years earlier. Cross an old bridge over the Longstone Leat, now supplying water to several farms in the area. Pass a Scout Hut in the trees and cross a bridge beside Burcombe Ford to reach a small parking area.

9. At the far end of the parking area turn left across the grassy moorland towards Gutter Tor and a metal gate in the corner of a wall and fence. Turn right at the gate to walk up towards Gutter Tor beside an old wall. At the top, keep the fence on the right to go over a stile towards a trig point. Although these are no longer used by the Ordnance Survey there is a plaque on this one noting that it is maintained by the Dartmoor Search and Rescue Group.

10. From the trig point take the right of two grassy paths across Ringmoor Down towards the tops of the trees around Ringmoor Cottage which are just visible. On the right you will see Sheepstor church in the valley and the water of Burrator Reservoir beyond. You should be able to see the breakwater in Plymouth Sound and, on a clear day, the lighthouse on the dangerous Eddystone Rocks, 14 miles (22km) out to sea.

There are several paths and tracks across the Down but the beech trees around Ringmoor Cottage are a landmark. Keep going forward towards them and, when almost there, bear left down to the stile that we crossed at the beginning of the walk.

13 PRINCETOWN, SWELL TOR AND CRAZYWELL POOL

A walk with fantastic views from the highest village on Dartmoor with railways, rocks and ruins. Princetown's history is linked closely with all of these.

Princetown owes its existence largely to one man, Thomas Tyrwhitt. He was secretary to the Prince of Wales, later King George IV, and his vision was to develop the uncultivated expanse of Dartmoor. In addition to agriculture, Thomas Tyrwhitt also had his eye on the granite rocks of Dartmoor, never far from the surface as evidenced by the well-known tors protruding through the shallow soil.

Thomas Tyrwhitt thought that if the granite could be quarried and transported it would result in prosperity for the area. Construction of Dartmoor Prison started in 1806 and the village of Princetown began to develop. A railway was opened as far as the quarries in 1823 and on to Princetown by 1825. Originally it was horse drawn – an amazing feat as the line climbs from sea level at Plymouth to 1,380ft (420m) at Princetown over a distance of about 24 miles (38km). The railway later became part of the Great Western Railway (GWR) which followed almost the same route from Yelverton to Princetown. From the site of Princetown station, the highest in England until the line's closure in 1956, it is easy walking as we pass the ruins of Bronze Age hut circles beside the path.

Foggintor Quarry, which closed in 1906, is just a short detour from the route. However, we have a closer look at Swell Tor quarry, which survived rather longer, not closing until about 1938.

After striking out across the moor to Leedon Tor we go to Black Tor Falls, where there are two ruined tin-stamping mills beside the River Meavy. These were water-powered mills for crushing tin ore and possibly date from around the 16th century.

We cross the river on an aqueduct carrying the Devonport Leat and climb beside the cascading water up Raddick Hill. The cascade is 150ft (45m) high and is the only hard part of the walk. Soon after we visit Crazywell Pool. This hidden pool is impossible to see from a distance and there are all sorts of stories and legends about it, enough to fill a book.

Passing Crazywell Cross, one of many which marked the old monks' path from Buckfast Abbey to Tavistock and Buckland Abbeys, we follow good tracks to South Hessary Tor and back to Princetown.

THE BASICS

Distance: 9½ miles / 15km

Gradient: Easy gradients apart from one steep climb up Raddick Hill

Severity: Moderate

Time: 4½ hours

Stiles: None

Map: OS Explorer OL28 (Dartmoor)

Path description: Old railway track, stony tracks and some open moorland

Start point: Princetown village centre (GR SX 590735)

Parking: Pay and display car park in centre of Princetown (PL20 6QF)

Dog friendly: Yes, but keep on leads when near animals

Public toilets: At start

Nearest food: Several pubs and cafés in Princetown

Shorter walk near here: Walks for All Ages on Dartmoor - Walk 14

13 PRINCETOWN, SWELL TOR AND CRAZYWELL POOL

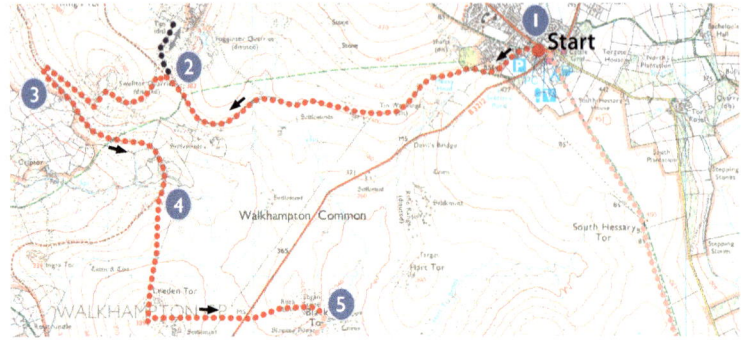

The Route

1. Turn left out of the car park entrance and walk away from the village, past the fire station. Bear left off the tarmac road onto a footpath signed as 'disused railway'. The flat field on the right in front of the row of houses  was the site of Princetown station and the small building on the left is all that remains. Beyond the old station area is the modern Dartmoor Brewery and on the hilltop behind is the communications mast on North Hessary Tor, a landmark for miles around and rarely out of our sight on this walk.

   Follow the fence and after a short distance look out for several granite posts on the left, most of which are inscribed PCWW 1917 although some have later dates. We will see several more of these on the walk and they denote the limit of the water catchment area for Burrator Reservoir, PCWW standing for Plymouth Corporation Water Works.

   Pass a plantation of conifer trees on the right and it becomes obvious that the track is that of an old railway. Cross a small bridge where the disturbed ground on the left is evidence of old tin workings. It is also the source of the River Meavy, which we will meet later on the walk. Shortly afterwards there are a few hut circles on the left before the track enters a shallow cutting with more PCWW marker stones on either side.

   Just over a mile from the start the track curves quite sharply to the right and Swell Tor quarries are visible ahead. At this point the railway can be seen far below as it passes another small quarry at Ingra Tor. The track that we see is over 200ft (65m) lower and a train would have travelled nearly 3 miles (5km) in a big loop around King's Tor to reach that point.

2. At a path crossing go right for 200m to see the flooded Foggintor Quarry and the ruins of various workshops and workers' cottages. Otherwise continue alongside

a raised embankment for 150m before turning left on a grassy path towards Swell Tor. Take the second path on the left after just 75m alongside a line of reeds. (Do not go all the way up to the top). This grassy path was in fact a siding for the railway and will take us past a small quarry on the left to the top of the main Swell Tor quarry where it is possible to look down into the old workings.

From the edge of the quarry retrace your steps for about 100m and turn right down a grassy path beside a hawthorn tree and towards the quarry waste tips. This path curves around, joining another siding to arrive at the ruins of several old workshops and the main entrance into the quarry. Just past these workshops old timber railway sleepers can still be seen in the trackbed before reaching some finished corbels lined up on the right, looking as though they may be awaiting collection. These date from 1903 and were cut for the widening of London Bridge but it seems were surplus to requirements. Go left here across open ground to regain the railway track below.

3. Turn left to walk past the spoil heaps of the quarry before the track curves to the right through a small cutting. Just after the cutting, by a bridge over a stream, is an older bridge on the line of the original horse-drawn tramway. For most of the way on the open moor the GWR steam railway followed exactly the same route as the older horse-drawn tramway except where sharp curves were straightened out. This is one of those original sections of tramway.

4. Just before a substantial overbridge go left up the rather eroded bank and follow the grassy path past another solitary tree on the left. Continue up to Leedon Tor ahead and, as the path goes to the right of the first rock pile, keep close to it and then bear immediately left (before reaching the higher and more impressive outcrop). Go carefully down through the clitter (rocks and boulders) towards two tors below the horizon on the other side of the Princetown road, Black Tor to the right and the more obvious Hart Tor to the left. After a short distance look out for a boulder bigger than the others nearby and follow the grassy path from there down to the road. Cross over and continue towards Black Tor.

13 PRINCETOWN, SWELL TOR AND CRAZYWELL POOL

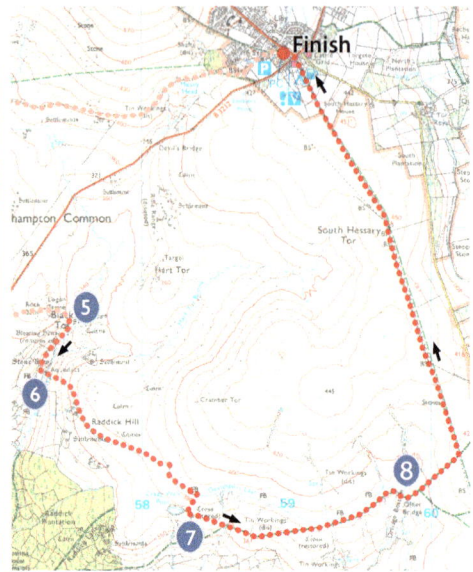

5. Black Tor is another tor which is comprised of several rock piles. The one on the left has a logan stone on top but whether it still rocks is debatable. Pass to the right of this one to go between the two larger rock piles and head down the slope directly towards Cramber Tor on the skyline. The path is faint but at the bottom it meets a more obvious track to walk alongside the River Meavy to reach Black Tor Falls.

   This delightful little waterfall is also of interest for another reason. Just below the falls there are the ruins of two medieval tin-stamping mills, one on each side of the river. The one on the far bank is better preserved but mortar stones, used for crushing tin ore, can be seen in both.

   Follow the path above the river towards the line of the Devonport Leat which can be seen ahead.

6. Turn left to cross the river on the aqueduct which carries the leat over the Meavy to climb up Raddick Hill. Here the leat appears to just tumble down over the hillside and it is a fairly steep and rocky climb to the top. Pass a sluice and two small clapper bridges. The leat negotiates a sharp bend with another sluice soon after. Cross the leat on the third bridge, bigger than the previous ones with three stone slabs, and take the grassy path heading towards Down Tor across the valley. This brings us to Crazywell Pool.

7. From the lower side of the pool turn sharp left towards Crazywell Cross on a wide, almost level, grassy path. Continue past the cross to join a stony track uphill. As the path levels out another old cross, Newleycombe, can be seen on the

right. Also in the distance on the right is the Devonport Leat contouring round the hillside.

8. At a place that delights in the name of Driveage Bottom splash through a ford and then cross the leat and up another stony track. Go left at a path crossing with another PCWW marker stone to walk along this straight path towards South Hessary Tor ahead. The path may be straight, but this does afford tremendous views in all directions as we approach the highest point of the walk.

On the top of South Hessary Tor is a replica of one of the boundary markers defining the limit of the ancient Forest of Dartmoor, the origins of which date back to at least 1240 when there is a record of a perambulation by order of King Henry III.

It is now an easy stroll into the village of Princetown where the Dartmoor National Park visitor centre is worth a visit.

14 TEN TORS CHALLENGE THE EASY WAY

THIS IS AN EASY WAY TO WALK TO TEN TORS IN LESS THAN TEN MILES ON THE WESTERN SIDE OF DARTMOOR. THE WALK IS NOT ARDUOUS BUT YOU WILL BE ABLE TO SAY THAT YOU HAVE COMPLETED TEN TORS.

The Ten Tors Challenge is an annual event organised by the Army for teenagers when teams of six will hike up to 55 miles (90km) over a weekend. Tors are a striking feature of the Dartmoor landscape and they come in many shapes and sizes. Normally these rocky outcrops are on the top of a hill and are due to the erosion of the surrounding land. The name 'tor' is derived from the Celtic word for tower, an appropriate description for some of the tors we will see.

This walk visits ten very varied tors. Starting from the popular car park at the top of Pork Hill we go to Cox Tor, the only serious uphill of the day, where the views are magnificent. The path then drops down to cross the old Peter Tavy quarrymen's path, used when men from that village would have to walk to and from their work at Merrivale or Foggintor quarries.

Two large prehistoric settlements are passed, the first below Roos Tor and the other on the slopes of White Tor. At a path crossing is Stephen's Grave. John Stephens was a lad from Peter Tavy who was in love with a local girl but, for reasons that are not recorded,

committed suicide in 1792. In those days, suicides could not be buried in consecrated ground and were often interred at crossroads so that the spirit would be confused. And so, the story goes, he was buried here.

The route takes us along a ridge with Roos Tor, Great Staple Tor and Middle Staple Tor. We bypass the smaller Little Staple Tor to avoid the very rocky ground there before crossing the road to Vixen Tor. (The walk can be shortened here by walking back along the road to the car park.) Vixen Tor is surrounded by a wall and there is no public access but perhaps this is just as well because legend has it that it is the home of a wicked old witch called Vixana.

Pew Tor offers great views in a different direction before walking back alongside the Grimstone and Sortridge leat to the cars.

THE BASICS

Distance: 9½ miles / 15km or 6½ miles / 10.5km

Gradient: Easy gradients apart from one moderately steep ascent near the start

Severity: Moderate

Time: 5 hours or 3½ hours

Stiles: None

Map: OS Explorer OL28 (Dartmoor)

Path description: Mostly open grassy moorland with several small stream crossings. Should not be attempted in poor visibility without good navigation skills

Start point: Pork Hill, on B3357 Tavistock to Princetown road (GR SX 531751)

Parking: Large free car park at start (near PL19 9LQ)

Dog friendly: Yes, but on leads if near animals on the moor

Public toilets: None

Nearest food: None on walk. Various options in Princetown or Tavistock

Shorter walk near here: this walk can be shortened to 6½ miles / 10.5km by returning along the road from Waypoint 9

14 TEN TORS CHALLENGE THE EASY WAY

The Route

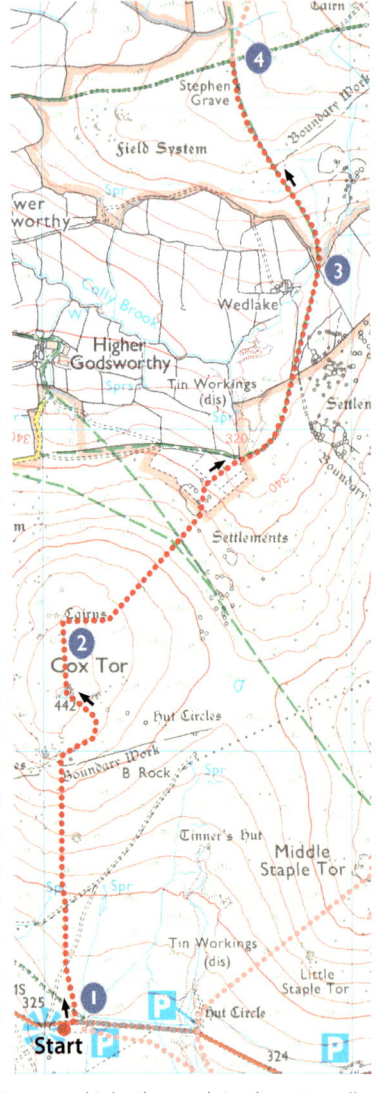

1. Cross the road by the car park entrance and go up a broad grassy track heading straight towards Cox Tor. The path starts very gently but near the top it steepens considerably past a small quarry. Cox Tor is a rock-strewn and fragmented peak with the highest point at 442m (1,450ft) above sea level.

   At the top there seems to be a wall of broken rock but bear right around the piles of boulders to reach the trig point. From the summit continue forward towards a large cairn, the pile of stones of which is visible from some distance away.

2. Turn right at the cairn over grassy moorland towards Great Mis Tor on the skyline to avoid the hummocky ground on the left. After 200m bear left on a grassy path between the hummocks and towards the field enclosures ahead halfway between Roos Tor and White Tor. Soon the corner of another field enclosure which is rather closer will come into view. Keep straight ahead for the corner, possibly bearing left in summer to avoid the bracken.

   At the wall go right to cross a small stream and take the rough track past a gully. Veer left towards a gate in another wall. About 100m to the right of the gate is the Roos Tor prehistoric settlement with over 70 hut circles in the complex, although from a distance it appears to be just a jumble of rocks.

3. Go through the gate and follow the signed bridleway diagonally across the field to another gate in the corner. Ford the Colly Brook (or jump across a little further upstream) to carry on alongside a field wall. When the wall ends continue ahead in the same direction passing several large boulders. Eventually we reach a track, on the junction of which is Stephen's Grave.

14 TEN TORS CHALLENGE THE EASY WAY

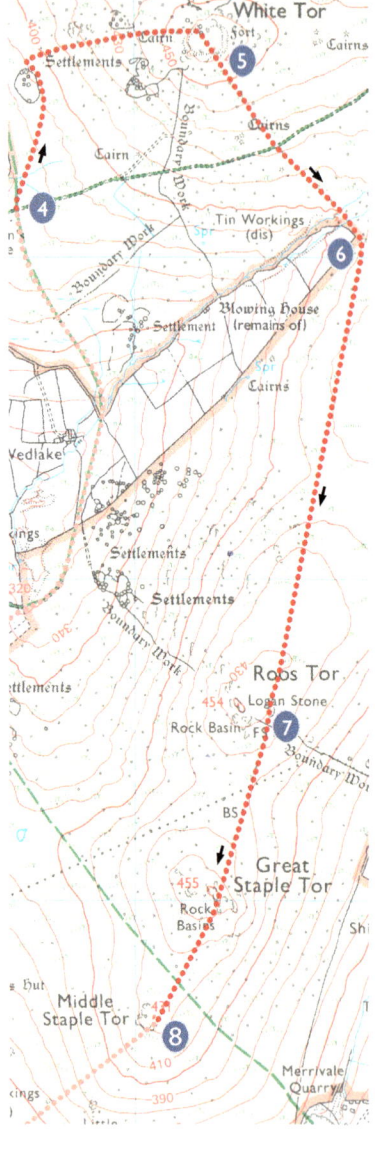

4. Cross this track to continue forward on a lesser one towards another field wall. At the corner of the field bear right, away from the wall, towards Little White Tor, the second tor. Before long we meet the boundary wall of another prehistoric settlement. Follow this and at the far end of the enclosure go right uphill to Little White Tor.

Continue towards the flagpole on White Tor itself. (The flagpole indicates that the boundary of the Merrivale Military Firing Range is close by. White Tor itself is not within the range so there is no problem even if the flag is flying).

On the top of the tor is what is believed to be the ruin of a late Neolithic hill fort that is probably over 3,000 years old. The double enclosure walls are now just a tumbled mass of stones.

5. Turn right at the flagpole and walk down the moorland towards the mast on North Hessary Tor and the corner of the field walls. Cross a ditch and a track and soon meet a rough minor track crossing two small streams.

6. At the corner of the wall is a Peter Tavy parish boundary stone. Take the faint grassy path directly towards Roos Tor bearing away from the wall.

Roos Tor also has a flagpole but, like White Tor, is just outside the range. Close to the tor you will pass a marker post with an incised B and there are others on both the left and right. These were erected by the landowner, the Duke of Bedford, in the 19th century and are an early form of environmental protection. Granite could not be taken from the area within the boundary markers thus protecting the skyline.

7. Go left of the summit and flagpole and take the faint grassy path heading towards the gap between the two rock columns of Great Staple Tor, looking almost like giant gateposts. Go between the two largest rock piles of Great Staple Tor towards Middle Staple Tor. Keep close to the large rectangular rock pile on the furthest side of Great Staple Tor and the grassy path ahead will be clear.

8. Go through the middle of the scattered piles of Middle Staple Tor. Care is needed for a short distance as there are a lot of boulders and rocks (known as clitter) below the tor. There is a fairly obvious grassy path which heads towards a small parking area just visible (halfway between the main car park from which we started the walk and the estuary of the rivers Tavy and Tamar in the distance).

9. Cross the Princetown road and take the grassy path ahead. After just 50m fork left towards Vixen Tor to reach a small bridge over the Grimstone and Sortridge leat. This leat was constructed to bring water from the River Walkham to mines near Horrabridge, a distance of 7 miles (11km).

    Do not cross the leat, but turn left to walk alongside it, through bracken in summer, to pass a second bridge and then a third which is a single slab of granite. Turn right over this bridge down the wide grassy path to Vixen Tor.

10. Vixen Tor is on private land so turn right at the enclosure wall as far as the corner. Go straight on and almost immediately step over a branch of the leat. Turn left on a grassy path to walk alongside it. Pass a single hawthorn tree and a rather muddy ford to reach a very large boulder in the stream bed a few metres from the field wall. Step across the stream on another conveniently placed boulder and walk towards a track going up the hillside beside the wall. Beware: the ground is sometimes wet around this point.

11. Pass a stone marking the boundary of Sampford Spiney and Princetown parishes and as the track levels out it skirts Heckwood Tor, where several blocks of dressed granite have been abandoned.

    Continue along this track for about 500m and fork right onto a grassy path towards Pew Tor. Bear left at a junction and continue up to pass to the left of the main rock pile.

12. Keep the tor on the right and go up a grassy path to the top between the two main rock piles which seem to defy gravity. Pause to admire the views and then go back to the base and turn right to walk beside the tor to another grassy path leading back up. (This is to avoid clambering over the rocks, which is an option).

    From here take the track on the eastern side of the tor (the side towards the communications mast on North Hessary Tor) that heads towards Middle Staple Tor and the smaller Feather Tor closer at hand..

    Cross the Grimstone leat again and go to the left of Feather Tor, our tenth tor. Continue on the path towards an old cross known as Windy Post. Where the leat divides, one branch of the water goes through a hole in a block of granite. This is an early form of water metering known as a bullseye.

13. Walk up the leat for 50m, cross it on a granite bridge and turn immediately right to walk beside the water. Pass the ruin of an old wheelwright's workshop before bearing left on the grassy path away from the leat and back to the car park.

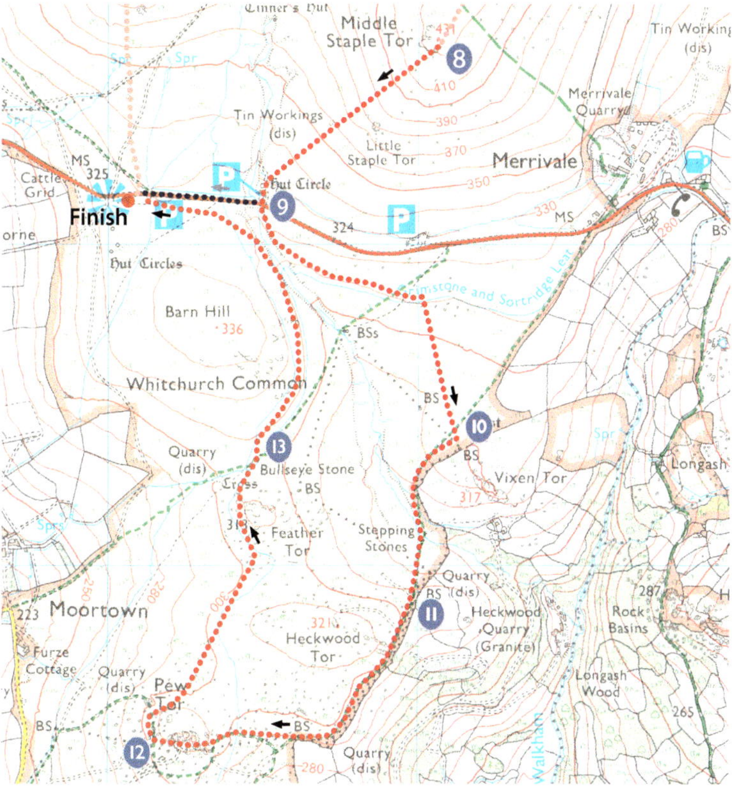

15 BUCKLAND BEACON AND RIPPON TOR

Buckland Beacon is a relatively small tor but, at a height of 1,253ft (382m) above sea level, it enjoys a commanding position and the views are tremendous. There is the added bonus that it requires only a little effort to get there.

Apart from being part of a chain of fire beacons in medieval times, Buckland Beacon is probably best known for another curiosity: the Ten Commandments stones. In 1928, the then Lord of the Manor of Buckland in the Moor, William Whitley, considered the rejection by Parliament of the proposed new Book of Common Prayer to be a victory for Protestantism. To celebrate this event he commissioned a sculptor to carve the Ten Commandments on two slabs of weathered granite at the base of the tor and they are there to this day. Although the lettering has been recut more than once the Dartmoor climate has taken its toll and the exact words are rather difficult to read today.

The walk starts at a road junction known as Hemsworthy Gate, although the gate has long since gone. The path up to Top Tor and then Pil Tor is easy and there are good views across the valley to the village of Widecombe-in-the-Moor below. Apart from its very grand church, sometimes called the 'Cathedral of the Moor', Widecombe is famous for its annual fair and the story of Uncle Tom Cobley.

There is evidence all around of much earlier habitation and at Tunhill Rocks there is a Bronze Age settlement, where the walls of a pound and of several hut circles can be

clearly seen. Foales Arrishes, another ancient settlement, is on the hillside below but rather hidden and obscured by bracken in summer.

Further on towards Buckland Beacon is Bowden Farm. This type of thatched farmhouse was once common on Dartmoor. Known as a longhouse, the building would have been shared with people living in the higher end and cattle in the lower part.

After the climb up to the Beacon it is an easy walk across Buckland Common before the final ascent to Rippon Tor for more great views in a different direction. Here we look over Haytor Rocks and towards Lustleigh Cleave. There are three large cairns on the summit together with an old stone cross on a block of granite only slightly raised above the ground.

THE BASICS

Distance: 6 miles / 9.5km

Gradient: Some ups and downs but they are not steep

Severity: Moderate

Time: 3 hours

Stiles: None

Map: OS Explorer OL28 (Dartmoor)

Path description: Moorland paths and tracks; may be muddy in places after rain. Short section on a quiet lane

Start point: Hemsworthy Gate (GR SX 741761)

Parking: Parking area opposite Hemsworthy Gate (near TQ13 7TT)

Dog friendly: Yes, but on leads if near animals on the moor or on public road

Public toilets: None

Nearest food: Cafés and pubs in Widecombe

Shorter walk near here: Walks for All Ages on Dartmoor - Walk 2

15 BUCKLAND BEACON AND RIPPON TOR

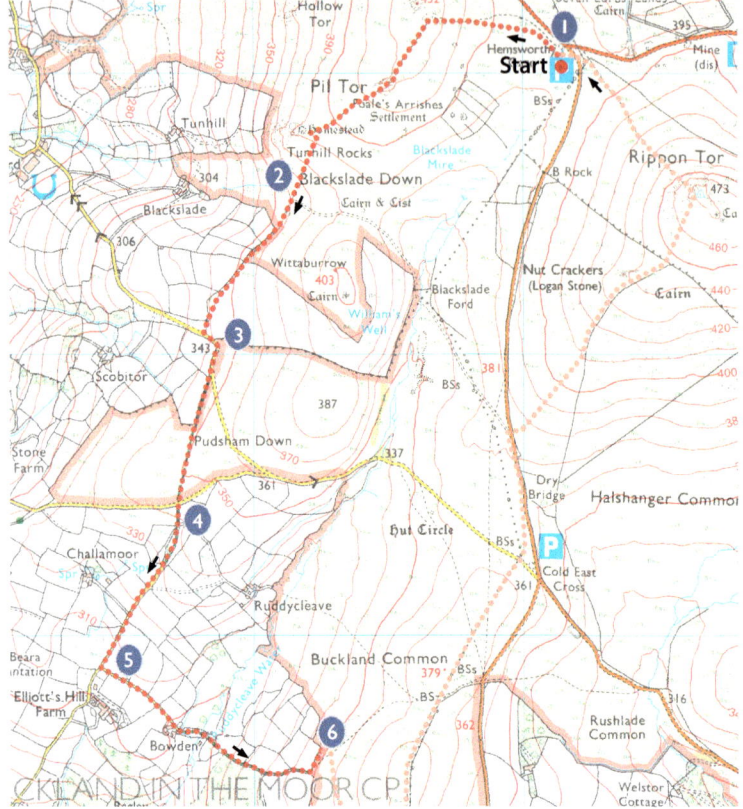

The Route

Hemsworthy Gate is an ancient road junction and before the cattle grid was installed there was a gate here. One of the gateposts has been built into the nearby wall and an old triangular stone direction post with the initials A, B and M incised shows the way to Ashburton, Bovey Tracey and Manaton. Over the wall to the north are the Seven Lords Lands, so called because at one time a Bronze Age cairn there was the point where the boundaries of seven manors met. Saddle Tor and Haytor Rocks dominate the view. On the other side of the cattle grid, in the corner where two walls meet beneath Rippon Tor, is a wayside cross known as Stittleford's Cross but now built into the wall.

1. To start the walk, go away from the parking area and the cattle grid on a clear path towards Top Tor. This tor is one of those known as an avenue tor, meaning that it has no single pile of rocks, but several scattered piles. Go left at the second pile on a level grassy path towards Pil Tor. This is another avenue tor and you bear right to walk between the rock piles. From there continue on another grassy path gently downhill towards Tunhill Rocks.

Here a splendid view of the East Webburn Valley and Widecombe-in-the-Moor, with its magnificent church, opens up. However, closer to hand and just as you approach the rocks you will be able to see the enclosure wall and a number of hut circles of the prehistoric settlement.

2. Bear left at Tunhill Rocks to walk down any one of several grassy paths in the direction of a small rock pile that is called Wittaburrow, with stone-wall-enclosed fields on the right. Beyond a solitary tree the path veers more towards the right and to the corner of a field wall.

   Continue forward with the wall on the right to reach a stile beside a gate. Go through the gate and just after some animal pens go through a second gate to meet a lane.

3. Go left up the lane for only 150m before bearing right on a public bridleway alongside a field wall and hedge. When the wall ends continue onward in the same direction as before on the track over open moorland.

4. Cross a road and go through a gate onto an old green lane, signed as a bridleway, with granite walls on both sides. This track is rocky at first but beyond another gate becomes a tarmac road between high hedges.

5. Go left at an unsigned T-junction before reaching Elliotts Farm. This quiet lane brings us to Bowden, a wonderful old Dartmoor farmhouse, probably dating from the 16th or 17th century. Bear left after the buildings onto the track to cross a bridge over a stream which glories in the name of Ruddycleave Water. Go through the gate and up another rocky green lane between stone walls, and with beech trees on the right.

15 BUCKLAND BEACON AND RIPPON TOR

6. At the top go through the moor gate and bear left to walk alongside the wall on the left. When this ends turn sharp right up a minor track, almost an animal track, and almost immediately go right again on a more obvious path. Almost at once Buckland Beacon comes into view. There are several paths here but keep heading straight ahead, at times through gorse and heather and ignoring any side paths, to reach Buckland Beacon.

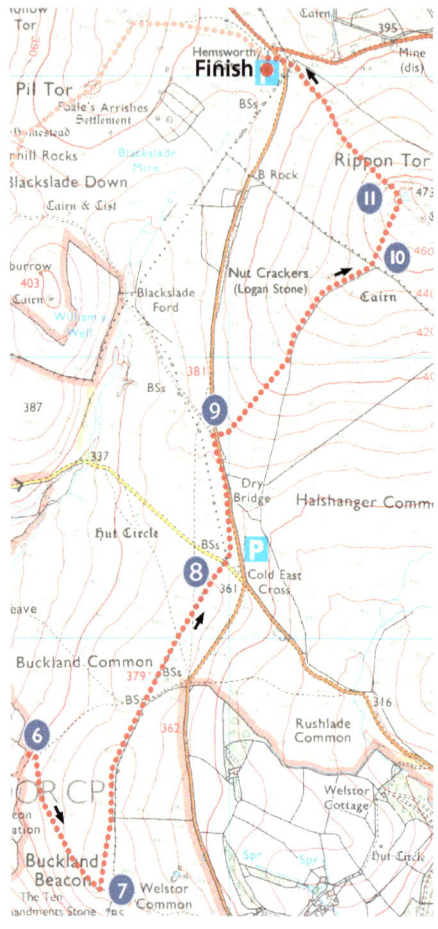

The climb is not strenuous, but it is worth resting a while at the top to admire the tremendous views in all directions. The two huge slabs on which the Ten Commandments have been inscribed are on the southern side of the Beacon overlooking the wooded valley of the River Dart below. In the distance, beyond the river valley, the outline of Brent Knoll can be seen beside the main A38 trunk road to Plymouth and Exeter, beyond which the sea is visible on the horizon.

On the right, in the valley of the West Webburn River, the church tower of Buckland-in-the-Moor is just visible in the trees and Leusdon Church can be seen on the hillside beyond.

7. Suitably inspired and refreshed, take the level grassy path away from Buckland Beacon towards Rippon Tor. Keep close to the wall on the right to avoid some boggy bits. There are splendid views over the wall beyond Newton Abbot and to the sea at Teignmouth.

   The wall curves to the right beside a boundary stone inscribed EPB 1837. The memorably named Edmund Pollexfen Bastard was Lord of the Manor of Buckland-in-the-Moor at that time and had a series of marker posts erected on the boundary of his lands. We now pass several more as we follow the path ahead (not continuing right alongside the wall) towards Rippon Tor. The path is straight, although not as wide and clear as previously, as it goes through the gorse and heather. When the path forks, bear right, still following the line of boundary posts and towards Rippon Tor. Look to the right and on the skyline can be seen a large brick building. This massive structure, seemingly out of place in the middle of the moor, is part of a rifle range set up during the Second World War.

8. Cross a lane and bear left past a small parking area to continue on the wide grassy verge alongside the Widecombe to Ashburton road. To the left is another boundary stone, doubling as a parish boundary with A for Ashburton and B for Buckland incised in addition to EPB. Continue towards an old stone bridge, shown as Dry Bridge on the map, and you will see one last boundary marker on the left. This post is taller than the others, and inscribed PW 1746. Philip Woodley was Lord of the adjoining Manor of Halshanger.

9. About 100m beyond the bridge cross the road to go through a gate in the wall on the right. Bear left up the hill away from the road on a good grassy track. This goes steadily uphill over moorland but soon meets a wall and a wire fence. Continue alongside the fence passing a pile of rocks on the left. These are known as the Nut Crackers and once there was a logan stone here but it no longer rocks.

10. Go through a gate and continue upwards to Rippon Tor. Turn around, and across the moor towards Top Tor and Pil Tor you should now be able to make out the clear outline of Foales Arrishes. The boundary walls of this ancient settlement are not as easy to see when close up.

    Rippon Tor has three large Bronze Age cairns on the summit. Go left between the first outcrop and the large pile of stones making up one of the cairns and with a modern trig point on top to a viewpoint overlooking Saddle Tor and Haytor Rocks. Further right is the Teign Estuary and the sea at Teignmouth.

11. From here the grassy path down to Hemsworthy Gate and the cars is clearly visible.

16 HAYTOR DOWN

An easy walk on Haytor Down along two sections of the historic granite tramway. There are Bronze Age hut circles, an old quarry, now a nature reserve, and great views.

Although it is nowhere near the highest of Dartmoor's tors, Haytor Rocks is certainly one of the most imposing. Arguably, it is the best known as it can be seen for miles around and is close to a road.

Haytor was also a very busy place nearly 200 years ago but for very different reasons. The granite here is of extremely good quality and harder than other granites found elsewhere in England or Scotland. The big difficulty was transport because Haytor Down is almost 1,500 ft (450m) above sea level. The Victorians came up with a solution, which was to build a horse-drawn tramway to connect with a canal and thence to the sea.

George Templer owned the quarries and in 1820 constructed the Haytor Granite Tramway. The tramway is unusual, if not unique, in that the 'rails' were formed of granite. The granite sections were shaped to guide the wheels of the horse-drawn wagons, which had plain iron

wheels without flanges. This meant that they could be manoeuvred at the terminals more easily. Teams of horses, as many as 18, pulled the loaded trucks up from the quarries and then gravity took over for the 7 miles (11km) to the canal basin. The Stover Canal had been built in 1792 by George's father, James, to carry clay for export from his land near Kingsteignton. The granite was then transferred to barges on the canal and taken to Teignmouth for loading on to sea-going ships. The empty trucks were then pulled back up by the horses.

After visiting Haytor Rocks we will leave the crowds behind to visit one of the smaller quarries before walking a section of the granite tramway. We continue across the open expanse of Haytor Down to the summit of Black Hill past the remains of human activity during the Bronze Age, probably 3,500 years earlier.

Later we walk along another fine section of the old granite tramway. As we approach the end of the walk we will see a hotel in the trees below. It was here that Agatha Christie stayed in 1916 and was inspired to write her first novel, The ***Mysterious Affair at Styles***.

THE BASICS

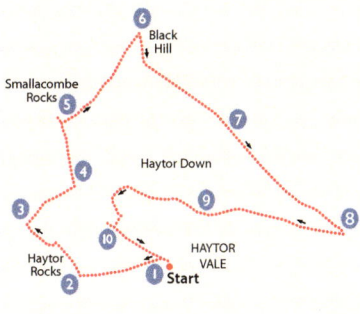

Distance: 6 miles / 9.5km
Gradient: Easy gradients
Severity: Leisurely
Time: 3 hours
Stiles: None
Map: OS Explorer OL28 (Dartmoor)
Path description: Moorland paths and tracks
Start point: Haytor Dartmoor National Park Information Centre (GR SX 765772)
Parking: Adjacent to the Information Centre. Honesty box (TQ13 9XP)
Dog friendly: Yes, but on leads when near animals on the moor
Public toilets: At start
Nearest food: Rock Inn at Haytor Vale or cafés and pubs in Widecombe
Shorter walk near here: Walks for All Ages on Dartmoor - Walk 1

16 HAYTOR DOWN

The Route

1. From the visitor centre car park cross the road and head up the wide grassy path to the majestic Haytor Rocks immediately ahead. Go to the left of the tor and then to the right of the second outcrop. As we have seen on other walks, Haytor has a distinctive double-humped profile from a distance but close up it is obvious that there are in fact two distinct and very large rock outcrops.

   Turn around for views over Newton Abbot, the Teign Estuary and the sea at Teignmouth, to the right of which the South Devon countryside stretches towards Torbay.

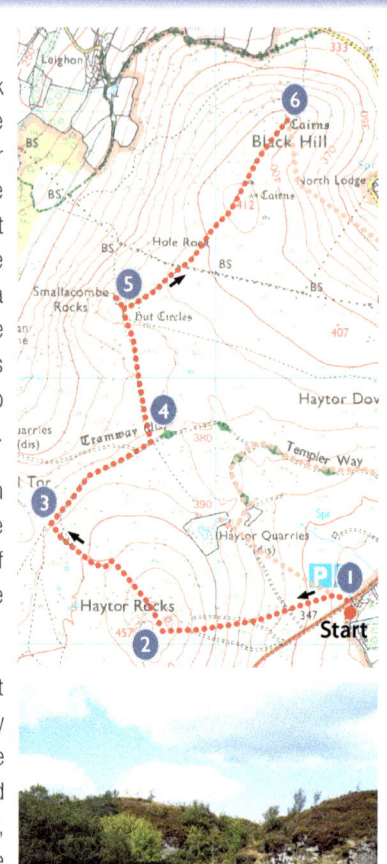

2. Take the grassy path on a slight downhill gradient towards the rocky Hound Tor in the middle distance and the rounded dome of Cawsand Beacon, 90m or 300 feet higher, on the skyline behind. There were quite a number of individual quarries at Haytor and the path takes us to the edge of one of the smaller ones, known as Rubble Heap. From here go left to circle around some of the waste discarded by the quarrymen. Pass the old tramway entrance through which quarried stone or waste would have been brought and continue alongside the spoil heap. Just past the end of the waste tip a section of tramway crosses our path beside a solitary tree.

3. Turn right, following the granite rails and passing a siding that went up to the quarry we have just seen.

Continue to walk along this level section where Manaton Church can be seen in the distance beyond Smallacombe Rocks. Pass another points junction to a siding on a right-hand bend; 250m later is a third junction where the tramway to the large Holwell Quarry joins the track that we are on.

4. Almost immediately after this junction leave the tramway and go left on the first of two tracks towards Smallacombe Rocks. Keep onwards, ignoring side paths, towards the tor but notice a large hut circle just before the tor itself. There are several other hut circles nearby although in summer they may be obscured by bracken. Continue for a short distance to the northernmost tip of the rocks for a good viewpoint. Looking left, the large Holwell Quarry can be seen and also the steep gradient up which the horses would have had to haul the granite blocks. In the deep valley below, the Becka Brook can be heard. There are extensive 180-degree views with the communications mast on North Hessary Tor near Princetown to the left and the town of Moretonhampstead to the right.

5. Go back as far as the large hut circle and turn left on a grassy path between small boulders heading away from Haytor and towards a row of straggly ash trees and a small tor on the horizon. On the slopes below can be seen Leighon Tor, rather insignificant as tors go and not shown on the OS map. Pass the rock outcrop on the summit of Black Hill and continue onwards to the cairn in the distance. However, there are three more cairns, in a line, just to the right of the path although again not easy to see in summer when the bracken is high.

16 HAYTOR DOWN

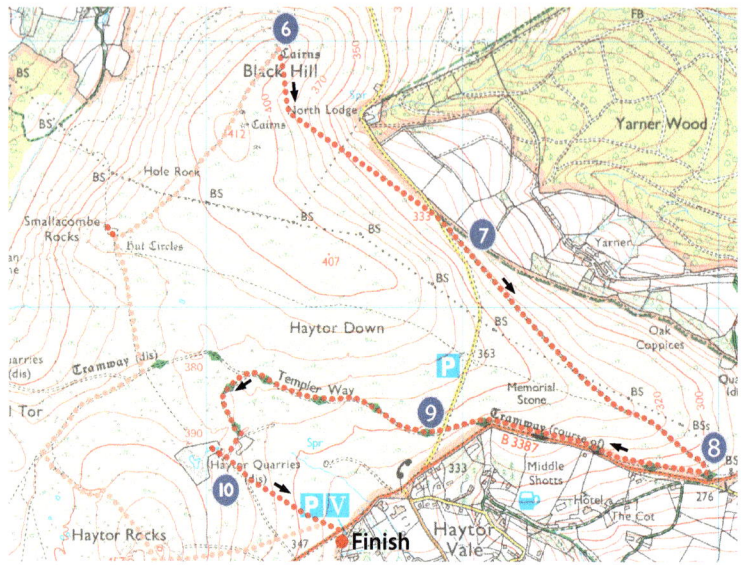

6. Go sharp right at the cairn, taking the first of several paths in the general direction of a minor road. (Beware, as the ground in front drops sharply away towards the valley of the Becka Brook.) The footpath can be seen snaking through bracken towards the lane but be careful as there are several other tracks here and some have rather steep gradients. Our path descends more gently to pass a few more straggly ash trees on the left. Continue straight on at a path junction towards the lane.

7. Cross the road by a small parking area and walk towards a cylindrical concrete structure midway between the lane and the stone wall on the left. Take the minor path past this which, admittedly, is not promising at first. Be assured that it will improve and has good views over the Bovey Basin to the left. Continue straight on at two path crossings by which time the path across Haytor Down has become broad and grassy.

Look out for a boundary stone, rather like a tombstone, inscribed with the name of the Prince of Wales. On Haytor Down there is a line of boundary stones erected in 1853 by the 11th Duke of Somerset who was Lord of the Manors of Ilsington and Natsworthy. These mark the boundary of each of his lands. Every stone had a name inscribed on one face, for example, Victoria, Prince Albert or Old Jack on one side and his initials, DS and the date 1853 on the other. There were over 20 set up and many are still in place and shown on the map. To confuse matters, this Prince of Wales stone is not one of the originals but a much later stone set up on the line of the early ones in 2001 to mark 50 years since the formation of the Dartmoor National Park.

Continue forward as far as a T-junction. Turn left here to walk away from Haytor on the broad path which soon drops down towards a fairly busy road at Green Lane End. There are views over Haytor Vale and towards the tower of Ilsington Church.

8. Just before reaching the road, turn right uphill on another section of the Haytor Tramway as it comes up from Yarner Woods. The tramway appears as a broad and smooth grassy path but no granite rails are visible at this point. However, it is not long until the rails appear again as we walk gently uphill towards Haytor. Just before crossing a lane there is a well-preserved points junction.

9. The granite rails are now easy to follow on the open moorland with the old quarry spoil heaps clearly visible ahead. Continue for half a mile (800m) to the point where the tramway forks and there is a stone identifying this trail as the Templer Way. Go left and follow the rails over an embankment crossing a stream and old tinners' workings. Bear left again keeping spoil heaps on the right.

Turn right just before some old conifer trees with spoil heaps still on your right. Pass the trees and ruined walls (ignoring any paths branching off on either side) and go up the slope towards Haytor Rocks. Surrounding the big trees is the outline of a collection of former cottages which were the homes of quarry workers.

10. At a path junction turn right and go through a gate in the fence to visit the quarry. This was the most productive of the various Haytor quarries from about 1820 to 1850. Stone from here was used in the construction of many famous buildings including the British Museum, London Bridge and Covent Garden Market.

Go back to the gate by which you came in and go straight down the broad grassy track ahead. After 100m bear left down towards the Information Centre and car park. It is appropriate that there are views towards Teignmouth, where the stone from the quarries was shipped all over the world.

17 HOUND TOR AND BOWERMAN'S NOSE

A fairly short walk with dramatic views, history and legend. Bowerman's Nose is an iconic landmark and surely the most instantly recognisable granite formation on Dartmoor.

The walk starts just below Hound Tor. This is one of the more impressive tors, although it is in fact several separate rock masses close together. Hound Tor is inextricably linked in Dartmoor legend with Bowerman's Nose. It is a long story, as many legends are, but many, many years ago Bowerman the Hunter was out with his pack of hounds when he was trapped by a witch disguised as a hare and lured into a trap. The witches cast a spell and Bowerman and his hounds were turned to stone. The result is plain to see to this day.

If that seems too far-fetched, it is a fact that Bowerman is a local name and there is a record of a John Bowerman being buried in a nearby church in 1663. It is, however, a certainty that Hound Tor medieval village existed and we pass the ruins of this settlement just below the tor.

There is a steep path down to the lovely old clapper bridge over the Becka Brook. The ancient bridge and old gateposts nearby show that this path was once a well-trodden route.

We pass close to Becky Falls before climbing to the top of Hayne Down. This high point, with views in all directions, is where we will find Bowerman's Nose. The granite rock pillar is a natural formation that, with a bit of imagination, could be human. It is so extraordinary that it has almost come to symbolise Dartmoor and is, in fact, the logo of the Dartmoor Preservation Association.

Towards the end of the walk we visit Jay's Grave, a well-known location and another of Dartmoor's curiosities. As with Stephen's Grave, which we see on another walk (Walk 14), Kitty Jay was a suicide and, as was the custom at the time, she was buried at a crossroads to confuse the spirit. Kitty was a poor orphan girl who fell pregnant by the son of her employer and was thrown out as a result. Rather than face the disgrace, she hanged herself.

However, to this day, there are always fresh flowers on the grave and at all times of the year. Nobody has ever been seen leaving them and some say it is the work of the pixies. Who knows?

THE BASICS

Distance: 7 miles / 11km
Gradient: Ups and downs, some fairly steep
Severity: Moderate
Time: 3½ hours
Stiles: One
Map: OS Explorer OL28 (Dartmoor)
Path description: Moorland paths and tracks and quiet lanes
Start point: Swallerton Gate (GR SX 738791)
Parking: Free car park at Swallerton Gate (near TQ13 9XQ)
Dog friendly: Yes, if they can manage the stile, and on leads if near animals on the moor or on public road
Public toilets: None
Nearest food: Seasonal snack bar in Swallerton Gate car park

17 HOUND TOR AND BOWERMAN'S NOSE

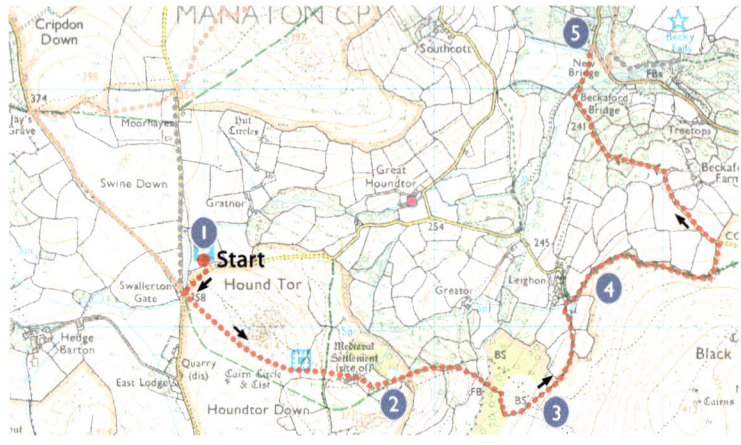

The Route

1. From the car park walk back to Swallerton Gate crossroads and turn left opposite the signpost up a wide grassy track towards Hound Tor. As the path appears to fork, keep left towards the right-hand side of the massive rock pile. You may need to use your imagination that this granite formation is a pack of hounds!

   It is an easy walk as the big views across to Haytor open up, and to the right across the relatively flat ground of Holwell Lawn can be seen Saddle Tor and Top Tor on the skyline. The moorland on the right is Holwell Lawn and is carpeted with bluebells in spring.

   Continue past Hound Tor on the grassy path towards Greator Rocks ahead. Take a left fork to reach a gap in a field wall by a rowan tree. At the wall continue onwards downhill (not the path going towards the right) to pass the ruins of Hound Tor medieval village on the left.

Unfortunately there is no information board to help interpret the ruins but it is thought that they are the walls of 13th-century farmsteads and were probably abandoned in the early 15th century. Why they were here is also a bit of a mystery as there is no obvious source of water nearby.

Walk past the village and bear right at the bottom of the enclosures through another gap in a field wall which winds through bracken to reach a gate. Before going through the gate, take time to turn around and admire the view of Hound Tor and the ruined village.

2. The path goes sharply down to reach a second gate. Care is needed here as the path downhill is steep and eroded in places. At the bottom is a third gate. The modern gate is hinged but you can see that the gateposts have slots cut into them. The old form of gateway used to be made by erecting two granite pillars, one on either side of the opening. Poles would then be placed in the slots. Usually the slots in one of the pillars is deeper than the other in order to allow the pole to fit into the deepest ones prior to being placed into the shallower ones. This is a good example but there are many more like this to be seen on Dartmoor.

After crossing an old clapper bridge over the Becka Brook the path continues through mixed woodland, weaving around boulders on the way. The Becka Brook flows into the River Bovey and then the River Teign to reach the sea at Teignmouth.

3. Emerging from the trees go left at a footpath junction. Our route goes between some birch trees and bracken (not the wide path going up the hillside towards Smallacombe Rocks). After a short distance it reaches a gate, beyond which is a stony track. This old green lane between moss-covered walls comes to a second gate and then to a path junction. Go straight on, uphill, signed as a byway.

4. After a further gate the track climbs up the side of Black Hill beside a field wall and views over the Bovey Valley to the left. Manaton's 15th-century church, with a tower that once was white, is visible and near the top of the hill Castle Drogo can be seen close to the skyline.

The track levels out at the top; at the corner of the wall alongside turn left down the grassy moorland to a road. Go through the gate beside the cattle grid and down the lane, with Hayne Down ahead. The lane drops steeply down towards the bottom and crosses the Becka Brook again at Beckaford Bridge to reach a T-junction at Leighon Cross.

17 HOUND TOR AND BOWERMAN'S NOSE

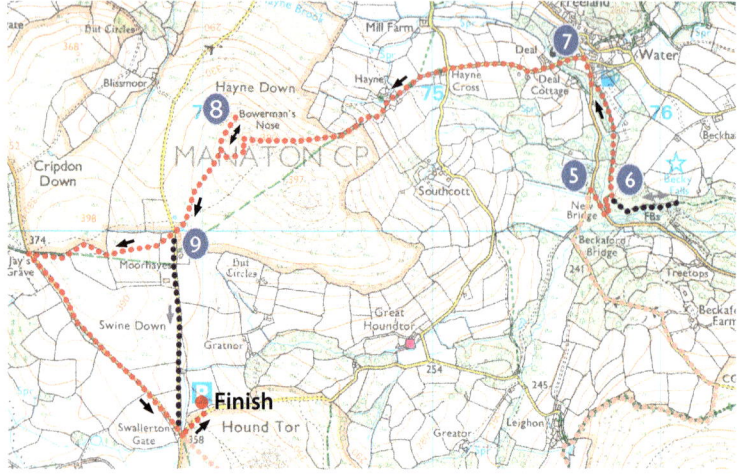

5. Go right, signed for Becky Falls, and walk along this sometimes busy road for just 150m before turning left on to a signed footpath just before a small bridge. (The footpath sign is small and not immediately obvious but do not cross the road bridge.)

   Continue ahead at the first path crossing to reach another junction signed as a footpath. If you want to visit Becky Falls, turn right and walk along this public footpath to reach a large wooden footbridge over the Becka Brook. This will take you into Becky Falls, which is privately owned and for which a charge is payable. Becky Falls has been a tourist destination since it was first opened to the public in 1903. The Becka Brook tumbles over a series of boulders dropping about 70 feet (20m).

6. Otherwise, to continue the walk, turn left at the T-junction and shortly afterwards go through a double gate, which crosses a nature trail, and onwards to reach a stile. Just over the stile on the left is a very old moss-covered clapper bridge. The path emerges from the woods to go around the edge of a meadow and then to a gate onto a road. Turn right past a row of houses and then after just 100m turn left at the crossroads opposite the Kestor Inn.

7. Walk along the lane and as it starts to go uphill there are a few interesting

old granite houses. Carry straight on at the next crossroads by the house named Sandy Meadow and up the narrow lane. Where the lane ends, pass a bridlepath sign showing the way to Hayne Down and bear left by a white house which is called Hayne.

Go through a gate and then steeply uphill. Near the top ignore a side path on the left to continue straight ahead to reach the summit of Hayne Down. There are several rock piles here but continue straight ahead to pass between the two piles in front of you. This is the northern end of Hayne Down and from the right-hand end of the ridge you can look down on Bowerman's Nose. For a closer look at this iconic and unique pile of granite take a path towards the left of the rock pile and after a few metres a level grassy track passes below the rocks to reach Bowerman's Nose.

8. Walk back from Bowerman's Nose and take any one of a number of minor grassy paths bearing diagonally across the moorland in a south-westerly direction to reach a gate across the lane below. A prominent group of conifers is the main landmark.

9. Go through the gate and a short cut back to the car park is to walk up this lane for just under half a mile (750m) to Swallerton Gate. Otherwise go immediately right on the signed footpath up the slope across the two fields that you can see. At the top, continue across two more fields following the hedge on the right to arrive at another lane.

Immediately opposite, where an old green lane goes down to Natsworthy, is Jay's Grave. There are certain to be fresh flowers, and possibly a few coins, on the grave. From the grave walk along the wide verge to return to Swallerton Gate. The thatched house at the road junction was once a pub. One wonders today where all the customers could have lived.

18 GRIMSPOUND AND HAMEL DOWN

This moorland walk takes us to one of the best viewpoints on this part of Dartmoor before visiting a prehistoric village, a medieval farming settlement and more recent tin-mining remains.

Grimspound is surely the best known and most visited prehistoric settlement on Dartmoor, as it is close to a road. This Bronze Age village is probably 3,000 years old and, although it has been partially restored, is in a good state of preservation. There are 24 hut circles enclosed within a substantial perimeter wall and with a stream providing a water supply running through it. It must have been a farming community as the site would be impossible to defend with high ground on three sides.

The walk does not approach Grimspound from the usual direction, but from the lofty height of Hamel Down. We get a bird's eye view of what must have been a busy place all those years ago before going downhill to explore the site.

But first we visit the nearby RAF memorial. This commemorates the loss of a bomber aircraft which crashed into the hillside in March 1941, killing the four crew members. Hamel Down itself has other reminders of World War II. There are a few decayed timber posts, all that is left of a wartime defence against an airborne invasion. It was feared that enemy gliders would have been able to land on this relatively flat expanse of moorland. There are tremendous views from Hamel Down which, at 530m (1,740ft), is one of the highest points for miles around.

From Grimspound we walk down a quiet valley to the site of Challacombe medieval village. There are now only a few ruined walls, but on the valley sides the evidence of medieval farming in the form of strip fields, a series of sloping terraces, can be seen.

We then return by walking up a second valley past the remains of the curiously named Golden Dagger tin mine and then further remains of Birch Tor and Vitifer mines. In this now tranquil valley it is difficult to imagine that these tin mines employed over 150 men, women and children in the early 20th century.

At the end of the walk the Warren House Inn awaits. This remote old pub is the highest in southern England and claims that the fire in the hearth has not been allowed to go out since 1845.

BRADWELL'S LONGER WALKS

THE BASICS

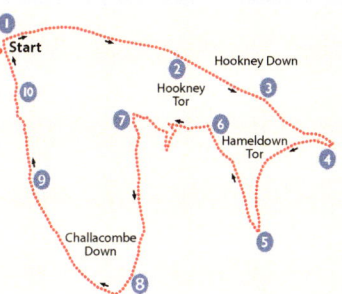

Distance: 8 miles / 12.5km

Gradient: Easy gradients with one moderately steep descent

Severity: Moderate

Time: 3½ hours

Stiles: None

Map: OS Explorer OL28 (Dartmoor)

Path description: Open moorland tracks. Should not be attempted in poor visibility without good navigation skills

Start point: Bennett's Cross (GR SX 680816)

Parking: Small parking area half a mile (0.75km) north of Warren House Inn (PL20 6TA)

Dog friendly: Yes, but on leads if near animals on the moor

Public toilets: None

Nearest food: Warren House Inn

Shorter walk near here: Walks for All Ages on Dartmoor - Walk 11

18 GRIMSPOUND AND HAMEL DOWN

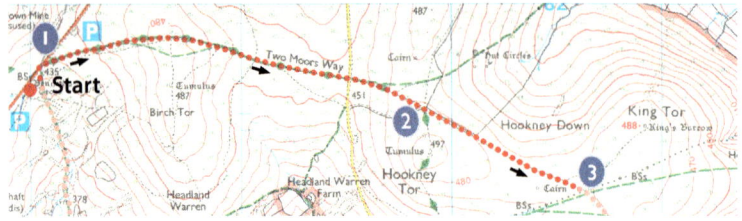

The Route

1. Leave the car park and walk towards an ancient cross known as Bennett's Cross. The exact reason for this cross being here is not known and neither is the reason for its name, although there are various theories for both puzzles. It is certainly very old and at some later date has had the initials WB carved on it. This stands for 'warren bounds' and it was one of the boundary markers of Headland Warren, a commercial rabbit warren that was in existence until well into the 20th century.

   Bear right to pass the cross and then left on to a sandy track, possibly muddy at times, up the hillside. Steadily climb, passing the ruin of what is probably an old tinner's hut on the way. At the top there are splendid views towards Moretonhampstead and, slightly left, Castle Drogo standing proudly above the Teign Gorge. Shortly after this spot another WB boundary marker is passed.

   Cross a lane and continue on the bridleway through heather and whortleberries towards a stone wall ahead.

2. At the wall go right through two gateposts and then left to walk on a grassy path with the wall now on the left. There are tremendous views over Moretonhampstead, Easdon Down, Haldon Hill and in the distance the hills beyond Exeter. The wall ends after 250m but continue forward in the same direction as before on the wide grassy path.

3. The path becomes less clear as it goes parallel to some of the anti-glider posts. Fork right on a minor path but beware, as there are no obvious landmarks. If you see a conifer plantation ahead and the distinctive twin humps of Haytor on the horizon you have gone too far.

   Continue on this lesser path towards a solitary wooden pole on the skyline and bear left at a junction with a better path. This good path curves around to the right and when Haytor is directly ahead take a further grassy path on the right to a single large boulder. This is the RAF memorial with a plaque on one side and the initials of the airmen killed on the other.

4. From the memorial stone take the wide grassy path uphill and follow this to the top of Hamel Down, where there is a large mound on the right of the path. This

is Broad Barrow, one of thirteen cairns along this ridge. Climb to the top of the cairn, where there is a boundary stone (with the spelling Broad Burrow), one of a series of marker stones put there by the landowner, the Duke of Somerset, in the mid-19th century. On the reverse are his initials, DS, and the date 1854. There are several more in the area, some with curious names such as Blue Jug and Grey Wethers.

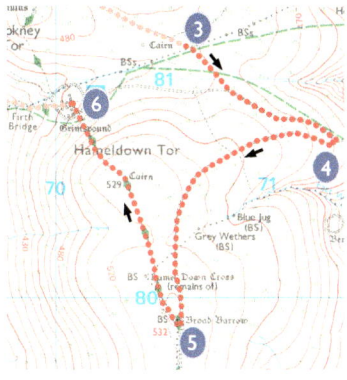

5. You will also notice that a footpath runs right through the middle of the barrow. Turn right and walk along the ridge of Hamel Down towards Hameldown Tor passing an old, but damaged, wayside cross along the way. This is Hameldon Cross and closer inspection will show that the Duke of Somerset had his initials carved on this as well. At the tor is another, smaller, cairn and a trig point. The path bends left before descending steeply down towards Grimspound. There is a splendid view of the whole settlement with Hookney Tor on the hillside opposite. Go through the substantial southern gateway and allow time to explore what was home to a lot of people all those years ago. Many of the hut circles can easily be identified 3,000 years later.

18 GRIMSPOUND AND HAMEL DOWN

6. Leave Grimspound by the lower opening and go down the grassy path, which has been paved in part to combat erosion caused by the many visitors. Cross the stream which flowed through the settlement and continue towards the road that we crossed earlier. As you walk down this slope you may be able to make out the ancient field boundaries on the hillside opposite, which appear as terraces. The whole hillside is covered in bluebells in spring.

Turn left on the road and after 250m go sharp right down a tarmac track towards Headland Warren Farm. There is another 'WB' marker stone on the bank on the right. There are records that there was a rabbit warren at Headland Farm as far back as 1780 but it had probably been established many years before then. At one time the enterprising owner diversified and the farmhouse became the Birch Tor Inn, catering for the workers of the local mines, some remains of which we will see later.

7. Cross a cattle grid and go left through the second of two metal gates, between dilapidated stone buildings. Continue on a grassy path alongside a barbed-wire fence with old tin workings on the right, beyond which can again be seen the ridges of the ancient field systems. Towards the end of the valley is a gate by some large trees. Pass in front of the cottages and through a further gate leading onto a concrete track. The substantial ruins are all that is left of Challacombe medieval village, abandoned centuries ago.

8. Pass a modern farmhouse and take the rough path uphill. On the left, beside a small pond, is a tinner's mould stone, into which molten tin would have been poured to form an ingot, and there is also an old granite trough. At a pair of gates go through the one on the right signed as a footpath to Bennett's Cross. The grassy path shortly veers right up the valley with the Warren House Inn visible in the distance.

Continue to a gate with a stile beside it and pass the remains of Golden Dagger mine. On the left you will see one of several buddles (for separating heavier tin particles from lighter waste), then the site of an old generator house on the right, Dinah's house on the left and the waterwheel pits across the stream.

9. Go straight on at two path junctions and up a stony and often wet track. The ruined buildings on either side of the path are all that is left of Birch Tor mine which was still producing tin well into the 20th century. Go straight on and when the path forks, go right.

This area, which seems rather rough and uneven to us as we walk through, was, for many hundreds of years, until finally abandoned just before World War II, a very significant tin-producing area. Two mines, known as Birch Tor and Vitifer, were extracting and processing tin for 150 years and the deep gullies are reminders of this industry.

10. Cross a stream and continue to follow this path through the old workings with Birch Tor on the right. It's a twisty old path but before long the car park by Bennett's Cross comes into view directly ahead.

Just a few hundred metres down the road is the Warren House Inn, steeped in history and legend. Over the centuries it has quenched the thirst of countless warreners, miners and walkers and has many a tale to tell.

19 CASTLE DROGO AND CRANBROOK CASTLE

CASTLE DROGO, THE LAST CASTLE BUILT IN ENGLAND, STANDS HIGH ABOVE THE TEIGN GORGE. CRANBROOK CASTLE IS AN IRON AGE HILLFORT ON THE OTHER SIDE OF THE RIVER AND THIS WOODLAND WALK VISITS BOTH.

The construction of Castle Drogo started in 1910 and is a fascinating story. Julius Drewe had founded the Home and Colonial Stores and made a fortune. He had traced his ancestors to nearby Drewsteignton, and had the rather eccentric idea of constructing a castle. Edwin Lutyens, the foremost architect of the day, was asked to build it and what we see today is the result. However, against all advice, Julius Drewe insisted on a flat roof so that he could walk around and admire the views. A combination of this and the Dartmoor weather has brought many problems over the years. The National Trust, who now own the estate, embarked on a five-year project in 2012 to make the building watertight.

Our walk takes us from the grounds of Castle Drogo down into the Teign Valley. After crossing the river on a modern suspension bridge we pass a weir designed by Lutyens to supply a turbine house with water. This generated electricity for Castle Drogo until 1994.

We leave the river by way of the Deer Stalker's Path and it is quite a climb up to Cranbrook Castle on a domed hilltop. This defensive position, with 360-degree views, is probably well over 2,000 years old. Castle Drogo is across the valley and the rugged outline of some of the higher tors on Dartmoor is in the distance.

Later we walk beside the river and cross Fingle Bridge. This picturesque and very narrow bridge is thought to date from Elizabethan times and was once a major crossing point on the route of the old road to Moretonhampstead.

The return to Castle Drogo is along the Hunter's Path. This is possibly one of the best-known paths on Dartmoor and, as it features in almost every guidebook, is not to be missed. A steady climb up from the river through an oak wood becomes a relatively level walk with the sound of the rushing water far below.

Castle Drogo is unique and is worth a visit. Not only is it the last castle built in England but it is probably the last house to be built entirely of granite.

BRADWELL'S LONGER WALKS

THE BASICS

Distance: 7½ miles / 12km

Gradient: Some steep ups and downs

Severity: Moderate / Hard

Time: 4½ hours

Stiles: None

Map: OS Explorer OL28 (Dartmoor)

Path description: Woodland tracks, stony and rough in places, but otherwise good footpaths

Start point: Castle Drogo (GR SX 725902)

Parking: National Trust car park at Castle Drogo (EX6 6PB)

Dog friendly: Yes, but on leads when on public road

Public toilets: At National Trust Visitor Centre and at Fingle Bridge

Nearest food: Café at National Trust Visitor Centre or Fingle Bridge Inn

19 CASTLE DROGO AND CRANBROOK CASTLE

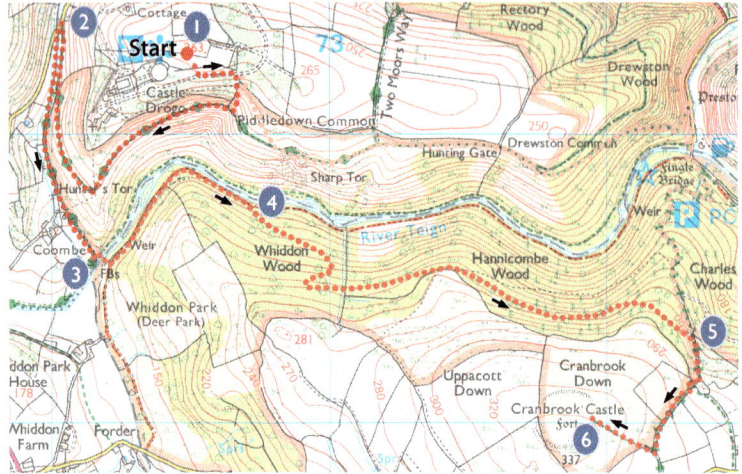

The Route

1. Go back to the car park entrance and walk up the drive for 100m. Turn right on a path going into the trees signed as Estate Walks to Fingle Bridge. Almost immediately afterwards go straight ahead at a path junction, signed to the Hunter's Path.

   Go down the steps to a T-junction and then right onto the Hunter's Path, signed to Dogmarsh Bridge. The hunter of old would have enjoyed the stunning views over the Teign Gorge towards Chagford. This path is part of the Two Moors Way, a long-distance route that links the north and south coasts of Devon, crossing Exmoor and Dartmoor in the process.

   As the track descends into some trees go right at a junction where there is no sign. The path continues downhill but if you look up at this point the massive building of Castle Drogo can be glimpsed high above, perched on the edge of the gorge.

2. Go through a gate and turn left down the tarmac lane. Take the left fork which is the driveway to Gib House (straight on is a private drive) and then left again just before the old thatched house itself. Carry on down through the woods to reach a path junction by the river. This is the River Teign, which rises high on Dartmoor and very close to the source of the River Dart and some other rivers.

3. Cross the iron bridge carefully – two previous bridges have been washed away! Go up the steps and over the wall and turn left onto a wide track. Follow the very

substantial stone wall on the left, covered in moss. The wall ends at a white gate with very large gateposts. Continue up the wide track that climbs above the Castle Drogo turbine house to drop down again to river level (although for a closer look there is a minor path at lower level).

4. Shortly after passing the turbine house, turn right uphill, signed as the Deer Stalker's Path, another obvious reference to hunting. This climbs steeply up through oak woodland known as Whiddon Wood and zigzags around two sharp bends, first right and then left, onwards and upwards.

Where the path starts to go downhill take the right fork signed to Cranbrook. The track, now wide and grassy, climbs further through Hannicombe Wood before levelling out. There are great views through the trees over the gorge and to Prestonbury Castle, another Iron Age hillfort on the far side of the river. Continue through the woodland, beech mixed with oak, before meeting another wide track coming up from the left.

5. Continue straight on, still uphill, and again signed to Cranbrook. Bear right at another junction, also signed to Cranbrook. After a while the track levels out and as it bends to the left you will see a footpath sign on the right to the Iron Age Ramparts. The final uphill section is a grassy footpath with bracken on either side.

It has been a long climb, but is there a finer view anywhere on this part of Dartmoor? Cranbrook Castle is almost 300 feet (90m) above Castle Drogo and there are commanding views in every direction. Looking north, the farmland of North Devon is spread out almost to the Exmoor hills and to the west is Cawsand Beacon (1,800ft or 550m) and some of the highest points on Dartmoor. Towards the south is the distinctive double hump of Haytor Rocks and Rippon Tor to the right. Eastwards we can see towards Exeter and the sea in Lyme Bay.

Bearing in mind that these ramparts are probably about 2,500 years old their size remains impressive. It is obvious that the early builders knew exactly what they were doing and took full advantage of the natural defensive position. In places the stone and turf enclosure, protected by a substantial ditch, is up to 20 feet (6m) high on the inner slope and almost double this on the outer side whilst enclosing an area reputed to be about 13 acres (5.3 hectares). The fact that the hillfort is on open moorland and not hemmed in by trees makes it easier to understand its huge size.

19 CASTLE DROGO AND CRANBROOK CASTLE

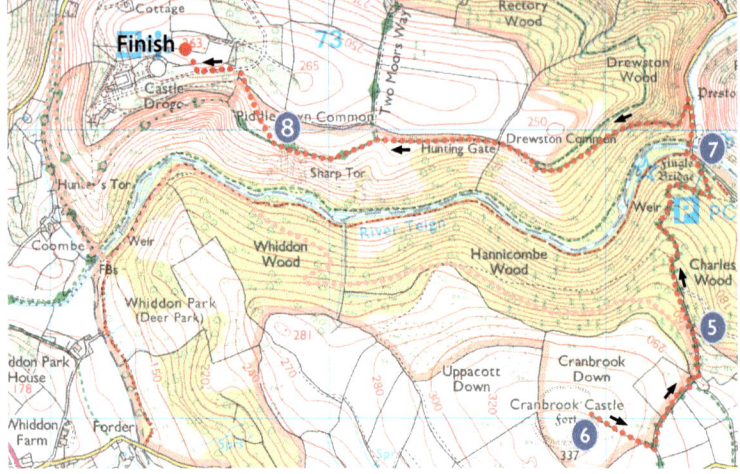

6. After soaking up the atmosphere and enjoying the views retrace your steps to Waypoint 5 and continue downhill through Charles Wood, signed to Fingle Bridge. Care is needed on the descent as the track is rather stony in places. Ignore side paths and keep going down on this old packhorse track to reach the river just before Fingle Bridge itself. Fingle is the name of the little stream that empties into the River Teign at this point.

   This narrow stone structure of three arches is a delight and in a most picturesque situation, hemmed in on all sides by the wooded hills. The bridge is very narrow because at the time that it was built, probably in the early 1600s, the only transport was by packhorse. The steep gradients and the state of Dartmoor roads was not suitable for wheeled traffic at that time. Fingle Bridge has, however, since then become a favourite with artists and writers.

7. Cross the bridge to the Fingle Bridge Inn. There used to be an old corn mill here which had a seasonal business as a tea room. The mill burnt down in 1894 but the owner of the cottage next to the bridge carried on with the teas and refreshments for the trippers. After more than one rebuilding this evolved into a pub known as The Anglers Rest, renamed the Fingle Bridge Inn in recent times.

   Go past the start of the Fisherman's Path alongside the river and continue up the lane for 150m. Go sharp left on a footpath signed to the Hunter's Path. This path climbs steadily through the oak woodland with the sound of the river below and eventually joins the Hunter's Path itself at a junction. Once out of the woods bear left to continue along the relatively level path high above the gorge and with Cranbrook Castle almost opposite. Pass the Hunting Gate where a wall crosses the path and continue straight on where the Two Moors Way is signed to the right. Sharp Tor, one of several with this name on Dartmoor, is on the left, high above the gorge. Down below, somewhere along the river a bit further upstream from here, is a pile of rocks known as the Pixies Parlour, but it is said that it is not wise to be there alone at night! As you enjoy the views it is not difficult to see why Julius Drewe wanted to build his castle high above the Teign Gorge.

8. When the path starts to descend take a right fork by some birch trees. The path is obvious but there is no sign. Pass a bench and then bear left to reach a gate. Go through the gateway and continue, bearing slightly right across a grassy area, to join the Castle Drogo drive. Go left along the road and back to the car park.

20 FERNWORTHY AND CHAGFORD COMMON

This is a walk, mostly on easy open moorland, from one of Dartmoor's smaller, but more remote, reservoirs. The area is rich in prehistoric remains and the route passes a fine selection of these, with tremendous views.

The walk starts at the end of Fernworthy Reservoir, which was built by Torquay Corporation and completed in 1942. We follow the water's edge through some of the fields that would have been part of Fernworthy Farm. The farmhouse itself was demolished when the reservoir was built, but some of the old field walls are still above the level of the water.

There is a whole complex of prehistoric sites in this area with a large number of Bronze Age stone rows, burial cairns, hut circles and stone circles to be seen nearby. The walk takes us past a number of these, perhaps the best known of which are the double stone circles of Grey Wethers. These two circles, very similar in size, are so close together that they are almost touching. It is thought that stone circles had a ceremonial function but why there are two so close together is a mystery. Later in the walk we will pass another single stone circle.

There is a burial chamber, known as a cist, on the edge of the reservoir. This example is most unusual in that it still has its capstone, or lid. Most capstones have disappeared and found their way into walls or other modern uses.

From the reservoir dam we walk across Thornworthy Down to Thornworthy Tor and then to Middle Tor and finally Kes Tor. Kes Tor, sometimes referred to as Kestor Rock, has a distinctive profile and can be seen for miles. It is also known for its rock basins, one of which is said to be the largest on Dartmoor. These are natural rock hollows and are to be found on some other Dartmoor tors.

From Kes Tor the walk takes us across the edge of Shovel Down, an area exceptionally rich in prehistoric remains and worthy of exploration. There is too much to see but we do pass one of the large standing stones and walk along part of a stone row before the fairly level walk towards the River Teign. An ancient clapper bridge leads to Teignhead Farm, now a ruin, which was possibly Dartmoor's loneliest farmhouse until it was abandoned in 1943.

THE BASICS

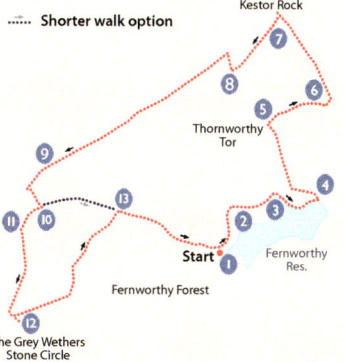

Distance: 8½ miles / 13.5km or 7 miles / 11 km

Gradient: Easy gradients

Severity: Moderate. Mostly on open moorland and should not be attempted in poor visibility without good navigation skills.

Time: 4 hours or 3½ hours

Stiles: None

Map: OS Explorer OL28 (Dartmoor)

Path description: Mostly open moorland but some forestry tracks. One small stream crossing

Start point: Fernworthy Reservoir (GR SX 659839)

Parking: Parking area at far end of Fernworthy Reservoir access road (near TQ13 8EA)

Dog friendly: Yes, but on leads if near animals on the moor

Public toilets: None

Nearest food: Cafés and pubs in Chagford

Shorter walk near here: Walks for All Ages on Dartmoor - Walk 6

20 FERNWORTHY AND CHAGFORD COMMON

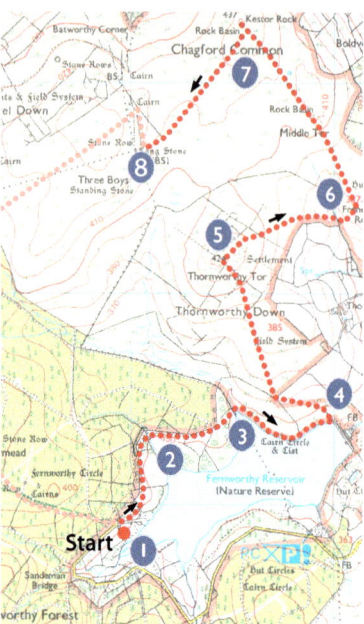

The Route

1. Go through the gate beside an old slotted gatepost to walk away from the parking area on the path around the reservoir. (Do not go up the forestry track signed as a bridleway – this is the return route). The level path shortly passes through another old gateway in a stone wall. Then bear left across the top of the grassy area in front towards a row of beech trees.

2. The path goes through a kissing gate beside which is an information board about the habitat conservation of the area around Fernworthy Reservoir, particularly for rare species of butterfly. Continue alongside the fence, with the reservoir visible on the right, to pass through a second kissing gate. Cross a long boardwalk over marshy ground and a stream. Then take the firm path along the edge of the conifer plantation.

3. Go through a pair of gates to yet another kissing gate before going down steps and over a footbridge across a stream. From here the path follows the water's edge and may be muddy in places. Look out for an excellent example of a cist (burial chamber) complete with a capstone beside the path. It is about 50m before a large conifer tree almost on the water's edge as the dam comes into view.

4. Turn left at the end of the dam to walk uphill, and immediately take the left fork. Cross two old walls and walk diagonally across open ground towards another wall and a line of beech trees. A post-and-wire fence is on the right. Go through the gap in the wall and turn right to walk alongside the trees to a gate beside a stile.

   Go through the gate and uphill across Thornworthy Down to Thornworthy Tor, clearly visible on the skyline. This is easy going on open moorland but there is no clear track. From the top is a good view backwards of Fernworthy Reservoir whilst in the opposite direction is the distinctive flat-topped profile of Kestor Rock. To the right of Kestor is Middle Tor, also above the horizon. Further right, but below the horizon, is a small tor that is named Frenchbeer Rock, and this is where we are headed.

5. Walk gently downhill towards the tor with fields on the right. Our way almost converges with the corner of the enclosure. There is no path to follow but the going is fairly easy as it goes gently downhill. Towards the bottom, as another stone wall is reached, keep to the right through some gorse to a metal gate with a stream beyond. Go through the gate, step across the stream and go straight ahead up the hillside to Frenchbeer Rock.

From here the extent of the valley dammed by the reservoir can be appreciated. The South Teign River is about 300ft (almost 100m) below as it makes its way through the steep-sided valley towards Chagford. Also look out for several very substantial hut circles on the far side of Frenchbeer Rock (towards the trees).

6. Take the broad grassy path towards Middle Tor, with the conifer plantation on the right. Continue onwards to Kestor Rock. Oddly the profile is not as flat topped close up as it is from a distance. The tor is notable for the several rock basins on the top, one of them the largest on Dartmoor. There is an easy way to the top on the north side and the largest of the basins is on the left. There are splendid views across mid Devon with Chagford and Castle Drogo in between. In the other direction can be seen some of the highest tors on Dartmoor including Yes Tor.

7. From Kes Tor, take the grassy path from the southern side towards Fernworthy plantation with other conifers surrounding Batworthy on the right. Ignore a track to the right and keep straight on towards a large standing stone. This has the initials DC, GP and C inscribed on it denoting the Duchy of Cornwall, Gidleigh Parish and Chagford and also marks the end of a double stone row. This part of Chagford Common is called Shovel Down and there are several more stone rows and stone circles in the ceremonial complex just a short distance north of here.

20 FERNWORTHY AND CHAGFORD COMMON

8. Turn right at the standing stone to walk alongside the stone row almost to the top of the gradient. The stones are rather small and partly hidden in the grassy vegetation. Turn left onto a wide grassy track when a cross path intersects. On the ridge to the right can be seen the profiles of Watern Tor and Wild Tor whilst the ridge to the left is that of Hamel Down.

Go through a gate in a stone wall and continue onwards with Fernworthy plantation on the left. After 350m look out for a granite slab just to the right of the path which is a memorial to a Royal Marine who died at this spot on a training exercise in 1992. On the hillside on the other side of the valley is the outline of a prehistoric settlement. From here the path can be rather wet close to the wall as we approach the valley of the River Teign.

9. Go through the gate to the right of a ladder stile and continue on a faint track through the grass towards the ruined Teignhead Farm which can be seen across the river. Soon the old clapper bridge over the river comes into view and the path continues ahead to this point.

   Don't cross the bridge but take the farm track away from the river back towards the plantation. Although rather eroded at first it improves as it nears a gate in the stone wall.

10. **To take the short route back go through the gate and continue straight ahead at all path junctions to Waypoint 13.** Otherwise, to visit Grey Wethers stone circles turn right on a footpath away from the plantation, and towards the track that can be seen going up over Sittaford Tor. At first the path is faint but soon becomes more obvious.

11. Go through a gateway in a stone wall where there are two substantial gateposts but no gate. Bear left on a faint track across the open moor to reach another stone wall. Go through the gate and Grey Wethers stone circles are immediately in front. Although stone circles are not uncommon on Dartmoor, and we will pass another one later, there is nowhere else where two like this can be found.

12. Go back to the gate (but not through it) and turn right to walk alongside the wall. Then go through a gate into the Fernworthy plantation. Bear left at a junction and then right at the next, going gently downhill on a good forestry track.

13. At a forestry cross roads turn right. At the next junction continue straight on. Just beyond this point, in a clearing on the left, is another stone circle and a small stone row.

   Continue straight on at the next junction, now signed as a public bridleway. Just around the corner is a gate and the parking area.

ABOUT THE AUTHOR

John Noblet has lived on the edge of Dartmoor for many years. As a keen walker he has always been fascinated by the landscape and history of his surroundings.

Walks for all Ages on Dartmoor was written as an introduction to Dartmoor, so that others could sample what John believes makes this national park so special. This second book of walks on Dartmoor is an opportunity to expand on the theme and to share the variety that the moor has to offer with longer walks.

John's working life has taken him to various parts of the country and he has walked in most of the national parks, but he says of Dartmoor that there is nowhere else he would rather be. He takes an active part in various walking and local interest groups.